A HISTORY OF
CRICKET

black dog

A HISTORY OF CRICKET

CATHERINE CHAMBERS

black dog books

First published in 2009 by black dog books
This edition published in 2011
by black dog books,
an imprint of Walker Books Australia Pty Ltd
Locked Bag 22, Newtown
NSW 2042 Australia
www.walkerbooks.com.au

National Library of Australia Cataloguing-in-Publication entry:
Chambers, Catherine
A history of cricket / Catherine Chambers.
2nd ed.
ISBN: 978 1 742032 08 5 (pbk.)
Includes index.
Previously published: 2009.
Subjects: Cricket – History.
Cricket players.
796.358

Original text design by Cunningham – Studio Pazzo
Printed and bound in Australia by Griffin Press

Image credits:
Cover, *cricket bat*, iStock, Cover, *cricket ball*, iStock
p 2, *Ashes urn*, AAP, 26, *Grand International Cricket Match on New Years Day*, State Library Vic., p 40, *Jhulan Goswami*, AAP, p 50, *Sri Lanka — small but mighty Sri Lankan fielder, Aravinda da Silva, right, attempts to catch the ball off the bat of South African Makhaya Ntini*, AAP, p 54, *Whole length portrait of 12 Aboriginal Australian men in cricket team*, State Library Vic.
p 57, *Australian Eleven, 1880 picture*, State Library Vic., p 68 & back cover, *Test match, England v Australia at Lord's Cricket Ground*, State Library Vic.
p 74, *1932/33 Australia .v England Bodyline Series. W.M. Woodfull ducks under a rising ball from Larwood, D.R. Jardine, the England captain, is at the left of the infield cordon*, AAP, p 83, *Shane Warne*, AAP, p 84, *Muttiah Muralitharan*, AAP, p 97, *Ladies Cricket Team, 1890*, Photo Library
p 107, *Australia v India, MCG, 01/01/1948 Don Bradman batting, Phadkar bowling*, AAP, p 116, *Dennis Lillee*, AAP, p 148, *MCG, 1936/37 MCC tour of Australia*, National Library Aust.

black dog books would like to thank Dr Brian Wimborne, PhD., B.Sc., B.Econ. for his thorough factual check of this book.

10 9 8 7 6 5 4 3 2 1

For Anthony King,
my treasured husband
and, of course, cricket lover

Contents

'So when does it begin?'

COMEDIAN GROUCHO MARX (1890–1977), AFTER STARING AT A GAME OF CRICKET FOR A VERY, VERY LONG TIME.

Introduction

Millions of people across the globe play the game and watch it for hours, days or even weeks at a time. They sweat under an Australian December sun, or shiver through cool English summers. Sometimes players run themselves ragged until the sun turns red in the sky. At other times, they hang around the outfield with the starry hope that they will make a match-winning catch.

So what is it about this sport that makes it so popular? Why do athletes suffer these agonies and endure these conditions? Well, there *is* only one answer. Cricket just has to be the mightiest, most noble game. The pinnacle of all physical, mental and emotional tests.

But how did it get to be the great sport that it is today? It took a rocky road, and an interesting one that is well worth reading about.

The Ashes urn — a symbol of the continued rivalry between the Test cricket teams of England and Australia.

1 Baffling BEGINNINGS

The game of cricket developed in England over many centuries, but we don't know exactly how the game began, or why. There are many theories and countless claims. Did Vikings really row across the North Sea to play one-day events on England's east coast? Or was it brought to her shores by travelling sportsmen from the Lost Tribe of Israel, clad from top to toe in whites? These are hopeful rather than helpful suggestions. One thing we do know is that cricket most likely evolved from some type of bowls or skittles game. And, of course, there is no end to the arguments about the origins of bowls and skittles.

All balls and no bats

Ancient Egypt can lay the claim to many 'firsts'. It doesn't seem fair that bowls and skittles should be included, but they are. And how do we know?

About 49 kms south of Cairo — between 5,000 and 3,000 BCE — we know that a young boy loved the game of bowls. He loved the game so much that when sadly he died he was buried with two bowling balls made from stone, and four from crystal rock porphyry. There was a moveable, marble bowls gate as well. His parents spared no expense, for they also laid by his side nine conical-shaped skittles sculpted in alabaster and beccia stone. Then they set the whole kit in a hall with a limestone floor.

It is quite possible that bowls and skittles spread both east and west from Egypt. Europe was no stranger to contact with this part of the world. Camel caravans carried rich silks and pungent spices all the way from China and India as far as the Mediterranean. From here, these luxury goods — and possibly games — spread west to Europe, including England.

By 300 BCE, Germany was enjoying a game called 'kegeling'. It was a very simple nine-pin bowling game with no gate. Nearly seven centuries later and still in Germany there was a game called 'kegel', which is the name for a club used for self-defence. The idea was to stick the kegel in the ground and throw stones at it. And the inventors of this rather rough sport? They were monks. The kegel represented sin and temptation and the stones were meant to knock that sin right out.

An irritating start

So when did someone first try to stop the bowler from hitting the target? Did a sneaky, spoilsport passerby just stick a foot out in front of the ball and think, 'That'll stop him knocking those skittles over! What a great idea! Let's make it into a new game!'

First a foot, then a stick, and finally, a bat. Sorted.

Although you might have some better and equally acceptable ideas of your own. Now, which nation is going to claim credit for sticking the foot out first?

Here are some forerunners to cricket — or games that just came and went until the big one arrived. There were not a lot of balls around at the time, so people often used a small stick to hit instead. Some historians claim these games are the foundation of rounders and baseball, as well as cricket.

Gilli-danda

Sport is about skill and fun. And the Indian game of gilli-danda sounds a lot of fun. Gilli-danda was played from at least 800 CE and still is today. A small tapered stick (the gilli), about 9 cm long, is placed in a crescent-shaped dip dug in bare soil. It is surrounded by a circle of about 60 cm in diameter scratched out with a stick. A player takes a stick 60 cm long (the danda) and hits the smaller stick out of the dip. He scores by batting the stick out of reach of the fielder. The batsman is out if the gilli gets caught.

Gilli-danda is a very fair game because fielders also have the opportunity to score. If a fielder stops the hit stick, then the batsman has to place his bat across the large circle. A fielder throws the small stick at the bat to get a point. There are many different versions of this game, depending on which region of India it is played in. But all this hitting and stopping and throwing does sound remarkably like cricket.

It is worth considering that the Indian subcontinent had almost 1,000 years of practice in batting and fielding before they played the English cricket game. No wonder they're so masterful now.

Lapta

In Russia, there was 'lapta' which was being played by at least the 13th century CE. 'Lapta' just means a stick, or bat. The game is played in a field marked with a large rectangular court. The sides of the court are parallel lines, and within these are other, smaller markings, or bases. There are two teams, each with 5 to10 players. One team supplies the batsman, who faces a bowler. Fielders stand at the bases. The bowler throws the ball and the batsman tries to hit it to the other end of the rectangle. Fielders try to stop the ball and hit the batsman as he tries to get to the other end. 'Brannboll' is a similar game played in Finland, but without the bowler. The batsmen throws the ball up — a bit like a tennis serve — and then hits it.

Cat-and-dog or dog-and-cat

This strange-sounding game was enjoyed in Scotland sometime in the Middle Ages. The idea was that a player threw a piece of wood, the 'cat', at a hole in the ground. Another player with a stick — called the 'dog' — tried to hit the cat before it reached the hole. Sometimes there were two holes and players scored runs by running between them, which sounds a little like cricket. 'Ball-and-brandy' was similar to cat-and-dog, but it was played with a crooked stick and not a glass of brandy in sight.

Tip-cat

This game dates back to at least the 17th century in Britain and was introduced by English colonists to countries throughout the world. The batsman takes a long baton and a 10 cm stick. He hits the small 10 cm stick up in the air with the baton, then he hits it again as far away as possible before it lands on the ground.

Trap-ball

This game dates back to the 1700s and was played in America and possibly came from the English colonists. 'Trap-ball' sounds a bit like warfare, and indeed its equipment could just have been based on weapons. A catapult launched a ball at the batsman who batted the ball into oblivion. A bit like a modern cricket-practice machine when you think of it.

Poison-ball

A great name, but what about the game? This game was mentioned in a publication in France in 1810 but had probably been around for much longer. A ball was hit through targets rather like croquet. If a player managed to get to the last target, he yelled 'Poison!' Other players could get extra points by hitting the triumphant 'poison-ball' in the next game.

These games certainly contained elements of cricket. However, there were other games much closer to the game we know today.

Stool-ball

This ancient game can be traced back to at least the 11th century CE. A player with a stick defended his 'wicket' from a thrown stone, stick or ball of sheep's wool. Then the player ran off to another wicket to score a run. But what was the wicket? Some say it was a three-legged milking stool. Others, that it was a church stool.

Some believe that the game was started by milkmaids in the 15th century in Sussex, England, while they waited for their men folk to return from the fields. Others claim that the game was played after church on Sunday with the church stool.

Now we have a game that we're beginning to recognise as a kind of cricket. So let's move on to games that sound more like cricket.

Creag

Sounds a bit like the beginnings of the magic 'cricket' word, doesn't it? However, it means 'fun' in Gaelic. Although a later game called creag-a-wicket might just have been the foundation for our esteemed game, we only know for sure that creag-a-wicket was played in front of a wicket gate.

Cric or cricc, or even crick

Sounds like an insect, but these names are a bit more hopeful. They are all versions of the Anglo Saxon word for 'crook', as in a shepherd's stick. And this stick, it is said, was used to hit a ball of oily sheep's wool away from the wicket, which was just a wicket gate that led into the fields. So that's that. Or is it? Well, no.

Krikstoel

It's Sunday and we're back at church. Only we're on the other side of La Manche, or even the English Channel, around northern France, Belgium and the Netherlands. Flemish-speakers are playing a bat and ball game in front of a krikstoel... a church stool, turned upside down.

Names such as cric or crick or kristoel can give us a clue about who created the game of cricket. But it is where the game was played that was so important. 'Boring' old geography led to the game we know today. Soils, climate and vegetation probably had more to do with cricket's development than anything else. In England, the most rewarding place to play was the sunny, dry south, where the counties of Kent, Sussex and Surrey lie. The land where sheep graze on short, tufty grasses that grew on vast chalkland hills and downs, where a ball would skid and bounce in the hard earth. By the Middle Ages, close-knit iron and glass-working villages were batting and bowling on those cropped grasslands of the Kentish Weald and Sussex Downs. Flemish cloth-workers added to the mix, weaving the sheep's wool and binding it up into a cricket ball during their lunch break. Villages became competitive as they stitched together teams. A chance to have fun in the field and perhaps a bit of a gamble broke the weary week. Competitive cricket was born.

'He played cricket on the heath,
The pitch was full of bumps:
A fast ball hit him in the teeth,
A dentist pulled the stumps.'
ANON.

2 Ban the BALL!

By the 1300s a distinctive cricket game had emerged among the skittles games of koyles and quilles. It might have been called 'creag' and other similar names. Some called it 'handyn and handout', which probably refers to bowling and batting. It was played with special enthusiasm by the farmers and artisans of England's dry southern counties. But they were not alone.

Right royal spoilsports

As far as we know, this cricket fledgling was a game of kings and possibly queens, as well as of the workers of England. For in the Royal Wardrobe accounts of 1299 (nothing to do with clothes!), £6 was shelled out for 17-year-old Prince Edward's pastimes. These included a game called 'creag'. The frustrating thing is that there is no description of the rules. But £6 was an awful lot of money in those days and lucky Edward must have had some great gear. Edward I (1272–1307) was also known by the nickname of Longshanks, which suggests he had very long legs. Let's hope he developed his talents as a fast bowler.

In spite of the vague 'creag' reference, there is a great cartoon of early English cricket drawn in 1344. It shows a group of fielders standing at the ready. They're poised behind the bowler, waiting anxiously for a catch. A batsman is lofting his bat, ready to swing at the ball with a backhand stroke. The tension is electric. The bowler is a woman.

You'd think from this cheerful image that cricket was on the road to greatness. But with no organised pitches, games were often held in churchyards and other inappropriate places. On balmy summer evenings, players were free to shatter the peace, and a few church windows, until about 10.00 p.m., when the light faded.

But were they really free? The 1344 cartoon was created when Edward III (1327–1377) was on the throne and threatening the game of cricket. Edward might have felt pressure from priests to ban the ball in sacred churchyards. But his chief reason for crunching cricket was that it distracted men from practising archery on Sundays and holidays. In Statute 17 of 1363, he comes down hard on cricket with a heavy mallet:

> 'noo governor of house, tenement or gardeyn suffer wyllyngly any person to occupy to play at the classe keyless [ninepins], halfe bowl, handyn handout [cricket!]

> or quekbourd upon payn of imprisonment by three yerys.'

Yes, three whole years in jail for any property owner who allowed cricket matches on his land. Edward was not an even-handed king, either. He chastised 'laborers and servauntys' for messing about with sport. But they only got six days behind bars! For once, the poor almost got away with having fun. Not that they had much time for it, what with all that ploughing and sowing and harvesting.

Cricket's Dark Ages

While Europe was emerging from the Dark Ages, cricket was plunging into a thick fog. We see and hear little more about the game until the reign of Henry VII (1485–1509). By this time, Columbus had sailed the ocean blue and discovered the Americas. Caxton had brought printing from Continental Europe and set up a press in London, just waiting to publish that first cricket report. But it wasn't yet to be.

King Henry had banned cricket, except at Christmas. Even then, enthusiasts could only play at the master's house. So no belting balls on the village green, or chucking them in churchyards. Henry was the ultimate spoilsport. But thankfully, his son, Henry VIII (1509–1547) was more fun. Sport was a lifestyle choice for the young king. He did very little else, apart from eat and eat, and drink and drink. (Oh, and have six wives.) But did he love cricket? We just don't know. At least he didn't ban it for 364 days of the year.

Bats not beer

Cricket was still played when Elizabeth I came to the throne (1558–1603), but she was no enthusiast. During her reign, 'krekket' fans from the southern city of Guildford played on the first pitch dedicated to the game. The local authorities had other ideas, however, and by 1593 had banned the bat yet again.

Cricket spluttered but it didn't choke to death. That early passion for something that was more than a sport in the end triumphed over all opposition. And in spite of more grumblings about slogging sixes over spires, church games continued. What was the attraction? Did bowlers find upright gravestones just too perfect a wicket? No, nothing quite so ghoulish. The answer lies strangely in a law banning churches from brewing beer.

Yes, that's right. Churches brewed beer.

This practice had gone on for centuries. What is more, priests sold the beer and put the profits into the church funds. But in the 16th century, a grim lot of teetotaling Puritan churchmen changed the rules. Beer was banned and, with it, a bit of jolly drinking around the church gates. So what replaced it? A spot of sport, which included cricket, after the church service. Was there any betting? We don't know for sure. But it could have been a way for priests to get that extra bit of cash for the church funds.

Cricket soon became as addictive as the alcohol. Village cricket in the churchyard became the bedrock of the game. Landed gentry played and so did their workers. It was a game for all, even though the teams of different classes did not necessarily mix. By 1600 competition was keen. There were organised fixtures and the game had started to spread. It was certainly important enough to be mentioned in an English–Italian dictionary of 1598, written by Shakespeare's friend, Florio.

There was even a kind of county match played in 1610, between the 'Weald and Upland' team of Sussex and the 'Chalkhills' of Kent. You won't find any match fixtures or programmes for it, but we know that it was held because it was mentioned in court 30 years later! Thank goodness for court records. For they chart the rise and rise of the early game of cricket.

Cricket and crime

Many historians believe that cricket was a game for children until about the mid-17th century. But the crimes associated with cricket before this puts a lid on that theory. Adults were belting balls and swinging bats in all sorts of places — many where they were not wanted.

Some of these crimes were against God. People insisted on playing on a Sunday when they were supposed to be in church. Or just after church, when they were supposed to be feeling solemn and reflective. And the rest of the crimes were still against God. Cricketers insisted on playing in or near the church, with its fine masonry, manicured yew hedges and delicate stained glass windows. Would they never learn? The following are examples of shocking cricket crimes during the 17th century.

- **1611** Bartholomew Wyatt and Richard Latter of Sidlesham in West Sussex were so determined to play that they missed going to church on the most important day of the Christian calendar — Easter Sunday! They were made to do penance and fined 12 pence each. In those days, that equalled two days' pay if you were a shepherd and a day if you were an actor.

- **1622** On 5 May, a group of players at Boxgrove in England's West Sussex were caught playing cricket. They were duly prosecuted because:

  a) it might break the church windows (glass was hideously expensive in those days and your average peasant couldn't afford it).

  b) '...a little child had like to have her braines beaten out with a cricket batt.' (Not sure that this actually happened, but it was a possibility.)

- **1624** At Horsted Keynes in Sussex, Edward Tye tried to hit a ball twice and struck Jasper Vinall on the head while he tried to catch the first hit. Jasper died. The verdict was misadventure. But it still took a long time before cricketers realised that double-hitting was not a good idea.

- **1628** Sussex was a very tiresome place to be if you were a cricketer. In this year, in East Lavant, Edward Taylor and William Greentree were accused of playing cricket during evening service. 'No I wasn't, Sir!' said Edward. 'Only *before* and *after* evening service.' It was a good try, but the two men were fined and told to do penance in front of the church's entire congregation the following Sunday. Very embarrassing. But they got over it.

But even these humiliating punishments didn't deter people from playing cricket. Perhaps the law led them to organise the game, with regular grounds and advertised fixtures. Or perhaps the gambling made playing really worthwhile. Some of the prizes certainly did. Especially at the 1697 game in Sussex, which advertised a 'great match' between two teams of 11 players each. The winners received 50 guineas, with each guinea worth a little over one pound — which was a lot of money in those days.

Whatever the impetus, cricket clubs began to form. It is claimed that the first was set up in St Albans, Hertfordshire, in 1661, although this has been disputed. More importantly, the game spread throughout southern England. It reached the fields outside London in 1700, when a match fixture was announced on Clapham Common.

It was a great beginning to the 18th century for cricket, which gained acceptance throughout the land. Its final seal of approval came of course, in a court.

In 1748, the court at the King's Bench decreed that cricket was here to stay because it was, '...a manly game, not bad in itself but in the ill use made by betting ten pounds on it...'

So the gambling was bad, but the game was just great! And it became the most popular sport of the 18th century.

Who fell in love with cricket?

Was it the flamboyant, gorgeous Georgian kings of England who fell in love with the game at this time? Or the new upper middle classes with money and time to spare? The wealth of many of these new-rich had been gained through the trade in slaves across the Atlantic. Was it the factory owner, who strutted around the smoke-filled city landscapes of the Industrial Revolution that made Britain so rich and powerful? Was it the poor farm worker, who lost his land in a flurry of cruel Enclosure Acts, where common land was taken into private ownership? Was it this displaced farmer who joined the hundreds of thousands in the factories and workshops of the big cities, bringing his bat with him?

In truth, it was all of them. From this time, cricket grew among all classes. Separately, for most of the time. Nevertheless, the game danced through the middle of the century, when clubs popped open like buds in spring.

3 King of CLUBS

By 1725 in the south of England, wealthy London aristocrats and gentlemen were busily setting up clubs and fixtures. Matches, paid for by gate money, were a riotous affair and a hotbed of very serious gambling. We have a scorecard that dates back to 1727 and we know there were umpires, too. And lines of spectators held back by cordons of rope, with touts and snacks vendors dodging in and out.

The London Club and the Dartford Club were probably the most famous cricket clubs in England during that time. The Artillery Garden Ground, then home to the London Club, hosts matches to this day, although in a much smaller, quieter way. Then, it was one of the most important grounds in England. In 1744 it played host to matches that had to follow the London Club's rules, which included:

- The starting team to bat or bowl has to be decided by the toss of a coin.
- The stumps are to reach 22 inches exactly.

- A single bail of 6 inches is to be laid across the top.
- The wicket-keeper has to keep still until the ball is bowled.
- The ball must not be hit twice!
- The fielders *must* appeal for a wicket, or the umpire cannot give the batsman 'Out!' [We've suffered from this rule of wild appealing ever since. But wait...]
- The umpire is the sole judge! His decision shall be absolute.

Now, with today's television replays and third umpires, whatever happened to *that* rule?

Pitches for the posh

In the country, landed gentry — dukes, earls and the like — showed off their wealth by creating cricket pitches within their own grounds. Many of these gentleman played the game, but hired good cricketers from the working classes, too. The professional cricketer was born. Some were tied to landowners, and forced to work for them in the fields as well as on the cricket pitch. Others were free professionals who gradually moved away from their lords and masters to play for clubs that were popping up across Britain. By 1750, organised cricket had bowled its way hundreds of miles northward, as far as the Yorkshire city of Sheffield, which hosted quite a festival of local matches.

Thank heaven for Hambledon

But the colossal game of cricket as we know it today was the brainchild of players from the small village of Hambledon in England's southern county of Hampshire. Its cricket club was founded in 1750 and the first ground was a stone's throw from a very convenient after-cricket drinking hole, the 'Bat and Ball'. And over a pint of ale (or two or three) the club's committee members became among the first to establish regular fixtures. Basically, to have a season that was repeated roughly year-on-year.

Crucially, they built on the London Club's regulations and drew up a firm list much like the 42 rules that we recognise today. Who were these committee members? Sadly, not the labourer and the artisan. These hard-working country folk still played with a passion but were not in the mix when it came to Very Important Meetings. Hambledon's committee was made up of gentry and noblemen. These upper-crust cricketers didn't establish cricket's laws in the humble 'Bat and Ball', either. Instead they made their decisions in the loftier 'Star and Garter' in London's Pall Mall in 1774, where a considerable amount of cricket gambling took place.

A game we recognise

So what did this game now look like by the time Hambledon had fixed its future? Well, the pitch was full of lumps and bumps, but looked much as it does today. Scorers sat high on mounds of grass on the edge of the grounds, making a notch as each run was scored. Forty was a lot of notches for a team to make in an innings.

The London Club's 22-inch high stumps with the same distance between them remained, as they still do. There was a crease. A real one, cut into the turf — not just a painted line. In here, the batsman had to pop his bat to score a run. And the bat? It started life as a kind of bulbous curved baton — a bit like a hockey stick. This was perfect for the type of bowling at that time, where the ball was more or less rolled along the ground, like the game of bowls itself. The bat became flatter in the 1770s, as batsmen faced the brilliant fast-flighted balls of bowlers such as Edward 'Lumpy' Stevens of Surrey's Chertsey Club, one of Hambledon's greatest rivals. And Lumpy's ball? It had seams, although not necessarily where you would expect them. The first six-seam stitched leather ball appeared in 1780.

So this is how Hambledon played its fixtures and established slowly the reputation of its club, and the game, throughout Britain. It produced some fine cricketers, too, such as John Small, a brilliant batsman, and Thomas Brett, a fabulous fast bowler. But the club's glory years ended when the 'last word' in cricket clubs formed in 1787. This was London's great Marylebone Club. So what happened to Hambledon? The 'Bat and Ball' pub still stands, and Hambledon still plays, although down the road from the original site. Nevertheless, it is England's longest-standing continuous club. Small, but etched in cricket history, it paved the way for the big gun.

Mighty Marylebone

The Marylebone Cricket Club celebrated its Golden

Jubilee in 1837. This fact was advertised on a poster, which is just as well. Otherwise, we would never have known that the MCC, maker of cricket's modern laws and punishments, and upholder of English cricket's petty class structure, began in 1787.

Before this time, a group of London's 'elite' played cricket in a hearty but disorganised fashion at White Conduit Fields in Islington. They really were proper fields, too, although it's hard to believe that now. In those days, Londoners escaped to green spaces such as this, away from the stinking, foetid streets of the cramped city.

The game of cricket became a great escape for the wealthy, when they had to stay in town for a while. It was certainly up there with hunting, shooting, fishing and other gung-ho sports played at weekends and holidays on their vast country estates. White Conduit Fields became the home of the White Conduit Club. Not big, not well organised, yet the start of something simply enormous in the world of cricket. But it wasn't one of the elite who moved cricket forward. It was Thomas Lord, the son of a once-respected yeoman from Yorkshire who had fallen on hard times because of his religion.

Good Lord's!
The story of Thomas Lord (1755–1832)

Are we returning to cricket and the church? In a sense we are. For the most startling thing about the man who found the MCC's final resting place is that he was a Catholic in a fiercely Protestant country. The Catholic Jacobite uprising against Britain's Protestant government in 1745 sealed the fate for the nation's Catholics. They became a tiny, marginalised section of society. Life improved technically for Catholics in 1778. In this year, the Catholic Relief Act finally allowed them to join the army, own land, inherit property, and generally take part in public life. The prejudice, however, remained. It affected everything they did, especially in the workplace.

But Catholics could always play cricket. And one Catholic in particular, Thomas Lord, played it rather well. Like Dick Whittington, Lord found his way to London as a young man in search of cricket glory. He left behind his Jacobite family in sleepy rural Norfolk in the east of England. Surely London's streets must be paved with gold for a young bowler with no money, no connections and the wrong religion?

Lord of cricket

By about 1780, Thomas Lord was an accomplished bowler and was selected to play for various clubs in and around north London. One of these was the White Conduit Cub, where he was employed not only as a bowler but also as general attendant at the grounds. He must have been a strong leader and a good organiser. In 1786 George Finch, the ninth Earl of Winchilsea, and Charles Lennox, later fourth Duke of Richmond, persuaded Lord to start his own private ground. A very difficult task, but there was a carrot at the end of this stick, for the Earl and the almost-Duke promised to prop up Lord if he lost money on the venture.

So in May 1787 Lord snapped up the lease on 2.8 square kilometres of mud and grass just off Dorset Square — just in time for the beginning of the season. And it was here that the Marylebone Cricket Club played its home matches. The lease was due to run out in 1810. But by 1809 Thomas Lord had already made his money on it, so was able to plan ahead. He took his venture to two fields in St John's Wood — the 'Brick,' and the 'Great Fields'. Here, the St John's Wood Club and the MCC joined forces. Little did they know the magnitude of this merger.

Green and pleasant land?

But, for the moment, the Industrial Revolution was about to spoil the fun. Britain was booming. Factories and homes sprang up in towns and cities all over the land. Canal networks transported raw materials and goods from source to sale point. And one of these waterways was the great Regent's Canal in north London. It ended up slicing through Thomas Lord's cricket ground.

The next move was a must, and for the MCC became permanent one. In 1814 the Lord's ground was established at the St John's Wood site that we know today. But for Thomas Lord, the move was too sudden. He did not have enough time to recoup his investment in the previous ground and was close to going broke. At his wits end, Lord decided to become a developer and turn his beloved cricket ground into a housing estate. This way, he'd get enough money to live off for the rest of his life.

The game needed a knight in shining armour. And at just the right moment, William Ward, a Director of the Bank of England, came galloping in with a fistful of spare cash, a passion for cricket and great skill with the bat. Ward saved the ground, which stands to this day.

And Thomas Lord? He retired happily from the MCC scene in 1830 and moved to Hampshire.

The Grand International Cricket Match on New Year's Day at the Melbourne Ground, Richmond Paddock. Engraving features the All-England XI.

4 From club, to county, TO COUNTRY

The 19th century was still a wild time for cricket in England. The game was trying to find its feet; to harness the best traditions and ditch the worst. The best was the club, rooted in its community, with a growing skill base that kept cricket improving and moving ahead. The worst was gambling, which had made the game popular in the first place.

But as clubs sprang up like mushrooms in the night, betting became a scourge. Everyone wanted a slice of the pie, which led to that ugliest form of cheating — match fixing. No club was spared from this menace. In 1817, the great MCC's good reputation was questioned when William Lambert was banned from the game for life. Should a game tainted by cheating be taken up by the nation?

Cricket and class

But money was not the only reason cricket flourished in the early 19th century. It was a magnet that helped small communities come together as players and spectators. Everyone could play — from artisan to aristocrat. But in many ways it still cemented England's rigid class structure and on a Saturday afternoon, as cricketers spilled onto the green, the divisions were clear. Wealthy 'Gentlemen', neatly turned out with their 'whites' and bats formed one team. 'Players' with their working clothes and one bat between them, formed the other. These Players were paid professional cricketers who came from the working classes. (They would never have been able to develop their skills working 12 hours a day down a mine or in a factory.) Thanks to the increasing popularity of the game, players benefited from the gate takings. But there remained a snobbishness about professional players that carried on well into the 20th century.

In 1887, a professional player, Walter Read, was chosen to captain England's national side. Sadly, this did not start a trend. Wealthy amateur selectors spent the next 64 years picking one of their own to lead out the team. The great English batsman, Len Hutton, broke the mould only in 1951, when he successfully captained England against India, and then the side that won the Ashes in England in 1953. Yet *still* there were grumblings among cricket's controlling elite.

So how did cricket make its way across England? And what made it grow as a national game?

A piece of earth

A national sport at top level needs national interest to attract the very best players it can. How could it attract the millions of poor factory workers in England, who had no fresh air to breathe let alone space to practise their cover drive and full toss? In the 19th century, industrialists and politicians conceded that conditions for the city poor were cruel. What was needed were some pleasant green spaces, and so the park was born. Public parks were founded and funded by wealthy families and individuals with a conscience. The first park was created by Joseph Strutt in the English Midlands city of Derby in 1839. It was seen as nothing short of a social revolution and from then on, parks studded the cityscapes of England like emeralds.

Local governments got in on the act and paid for municipal green spaces. As Victorian landscape architect Alexander McKenzie said, they became 'the lungs of the metropolis'. There was not only short, smooth grass — a godsend for batsmen — but also lakes for the ball to get lost in, glasshouses to get shattered, beds of flowers with lovely heads to break, bandstands — in fact a whole entertainment area for the poor to play in and for cricket skills to develop.

Like a snowball rolling down a mountain, the sport was unstoppable and ever expanding. But what carried players and their passion around England so fast?

The right track

In the 18th and 19th centuries the popularity of cricket grew, aided by some very helpful technology. In the 18th century the steam engine sparked the Industrial Revolution. In the 19th century it brought the train. The first true commercial tracks were laid in 1830: the Canterbury and Whitstable in the south and the Liverpool and Manchester in the north. Just one year later, the

Canterbury and Whitstable line introduced the season ticket. Passenger services were truly on their way, and exploded across the land and into Scotland and Wales.

Cricketers took full advantage. Fixtures were made with teams ever further away. Players and clubs moved from south to north and east to west. And by 1888 in the Midlands, the Birmingham and District Cricket League became the first organised club contest in the world. Meanwhile, interest in competition on a larger scale emerged. The counties of England began to draw together amateur and professional cricketers to represent them.

In 1864, eight counties put teams forward in battle. The games were a far cry from those ancient wind-blown contests high on the Weald of Kent and the Downs of Sussex. The success of 1864 led to counties forming committees. Together they thrashed out rules of engagement. In 1873, counties were obliged to meet strict agreed standards in order to take part in what became First-Class competition. By this time, cricket had become so important that the agreement on standards was commemorated by a special-issue postage stamp. By 1890, the County Championship, as England knows it today, was born. It was restricted to only those counties that could supply good grounds and keen competition. Those restrictions still apply — keeping First-Class standards high.

Bricks and bats

But what of England? Even before county cricket, so-called national sides were touring the country. Between

1846 and 1882 there were a staggering 19 different 'English' sides. Often, they competed against each other. For the most part they were organised by the wealthy gentlemen elite. But not all. For in 1846, William Clarke, a bricklayer and excellent bowler from Nottingham, formed the 'All England XI'. It was made up largely of the cream of the professionals, like the great Alfred Mynn, with the occasional posh amateur. The team was created not only to entertain, but also to make money and satisfy the enormous appetite for betting.

Clarke's Eleven toured England, playing an assortment of local sides, which were terribly enthusiastic but usually vastly inferior. So, to even things up a bit, Clarke allowed these teams to field 22 players, to make it more of a game. It's hard to imagine such a crowded pitch, but this tack was very inclusive and encouraged players across the nation to take up the game. In 1852, William Clarke at last found some challenging opposition in the shape of John Wisden, who later set up the publication of the long-standing *Wisden Cricketer's Almanac*. But earlier, John Wisden formed a rival 'United England XI' with his Sussex teammate, Jimmy Dean.

The matches between these two 'national' teams became the most exciting fixtures of the season and galvanised the game across the nation. And like the great explorers of centuries past, cricket organisers became inspired to look abroad for even greater competition. What a time to do it! The Victorian era of Empire had begun. England now had its feelers across the globe, its fingers in every conceivable pie. The world was England's honey-pot, and cricket gradually became one of its national symbols. Not in a dynamic way — for the game was long and measured — but in a quirky, eccentric way that helped it spread to other nations.

Alfred Mynn (England, 1807–1861)

Alfred Mynn, a star among amateur cricketers, was among William Clarke's All-Englanders. He took 1038 first-class wickets with an average of 10.22. His greatest haul was 9 in one innings and he took 10 per match a staggering 34 times. Pretty good. Mynn was known as the 'Lion of Kent' but he played also for Sussex and the MCC. This 133 kg legend was large in every way, including his spending habits, for he was bankrupted several times and once imprisoned for debt.

5 Cricket across THE GLOBE

'Looking backward, we could almost see, suspended... above the flat little island, the ghostly shapes of those twin orbs of the Empire, the cricket ball and the blackball.'
PATRICK LEIGH FERMOR (B.1915–2011),
AUTHOR AND TRAVEL WRITER.

'The flat little island' lies in the Caribbean, where England planted its feet in the 17th century and wielded its bat, in every sense. From this time England traded or raided across much of the known world, and there is evidence that her soldiers, sailors and settlers took an early form of cricket with them. But the game really took root a century later, when England began its quest to control a quarter of the world.

Cricket and colonialism

Cricket was quite beautifully formed in the 18th and 19th centuries. Just in time to tag alongside Britain's growing interests in lands that could supply raw materials to support her Industrial Revolution. It was also a chance for a Big Adventure, for Britons loved the thrill of going into the great unknown. And when they'd finished exploring, they'd build a church and a cricket pitch. Soon, British government reps, traders, troops, clerks and cooks snuck into far-flung trading posts, naval bases and eventually, whole countries. And this is how the seeds of cricket took root on a wide range of pitch conditions around the world. First stop: England's nearest and dearest European nation.

A farewell to France

The first organised team from England to play cricket in Europe never got further than Dover Harbour.

The year was 1789. The dashing John Sackville, Third Duke of Dorset, swung his lead-weight 2 kg bat in anticipation. His valet checked his cricket gear: breeches, high-collared shirts, buttoned jackets, buckled boots, jockey caps with gold trim. The Duke did a few knee-bends to check out his upper-class limbs.

He braced himself. I mean, what could be more challenging than taking a cricket team to the continent of Europe? Hopes ran high for a very interesting tour. His fine team of amateurs would face new conditions, fresh wickets, and unknown opponents. But for the Duke, not unknown territory, as he had lately been England's Ambassador to France.

So with great enthusiasm, the team set off for Dover Harbour and waited for the boat to cross to Calais. But there, on the quayside, their dreams were shattered, for the French Revolution had just broken out. *Le criquet* became a victim of politics. The shape of things to come. A sharp limited-over cricket match would have sorted it all out with no casualties. But it was not to be.

So how did the rest of Europe fare?

Cricket on the Continent

In the 19th century, cricket in Europe was concentrated in tiny pockets where English traders and government representatives set up their 'Athletics Clubs'. Here, football, cricket, tennis and many other sports were enjoyed by English expatriates (English people living away from England) and increasingly, invited locals. The game became a spectacle during the wars against Napoleon, when British troops in Europe played in front of the astonished passers-by. Surprisingly, some took a real interest, like the residents of Lisbon in Portugal, who witnessed a match in 1808 and immediately took up the bat.

The game in Europe ebbed and flowed and flourished in a rather dainty kind of way. But continental politics and combats froze the tiny clusters of cricket in Europe. Britain had no authority here, and little influence other than in private commerce. Cricket had no opportunity to develop as it did in Britain's colonies. And as Germany united under Bismarck, and Italy coalesced with the help of Mazzini and Garibaldi, it became clear that European nations were forging their own strong identities. There really was no room for a 'strange' British game.

The game of cricket did hang on in France throughout the 19th century. The French competed with England in the 1900 Olympics in Paris, where England won the gold medal for cricket and France the silver. There was little to say about the match, and the fixture was not repeated. Neither was cricket as an Olympic sport.

But today, cricket in Europe is growing at a brisk pace. The Netherlands, boosted by immigration from cricket-loving nations, now boasts a very competitive One Day International team. While in France, cricket has come under the wing of its government Department of Sports. The game is supported and nurtured in schools and clubs for both girls and boys.

Cricket across the Pond

William Byrd, a plantation owner in the state of Virginia in America, kept a diary between 1709 and 1712 — and thank goodness he did. For without it we would never have known about this, the first recorded cricket match in North America:

> *'I rose at six o'clock and read a chapter in Hebrew. About 10 o'clock Dr Blair and Major, and Captain Harrison came to see us. After I had given them a glass of sack we played cricket. I ate boiled beef for my dinner.'*

Byrd was obviously well settled in America. Many English were. Virginia had become an English trading outpost in 1607 and the first of England's colonies in the western half of the world. Many 'English' plantation and mine owners, professionals and traders considered themselves American. But they still played cricket, which was a national game until well into the 19th century.

Keen cricketers in Canada

> *'Ho Cricketers! Awake from your slumbers and prepare for 24th May!'*
>
> British Columbian newspaper, 17 May 1862.

Was this to be a great cricketing spectacle in a stadium with stands, bands and hollering fans? No. It was a match played on a pitch cleared of trees, shrubs and dried wood only a little while earlier. Canvas refreshment tents were dotted around the field. Ladies in flamboyant hats and floating gowns wafted among the officers and gentlemen. It was a festival as much as a jolly game of cricket. Although the sport itself, as in America, was of national importance for quite some time. It was so important to both sides that it started something really big.

The first international clash

International cricket began in 1844, and England was nowhere in sight. It might now seem a surprising start, for the match was between Canada and the United States. The enthusiastic Americans continued this as an annual fixture, and in 1859, England joined in the fun. One of the many 'English' sides took its first international tour across the Atlantic. But not long after this, America had other things on its mind. Sport, and especially the English game, got tossed aside. And this is why...

The northern states, led by Abraham Lincoln, wanted to prevent slavery from spreading upwards from the southern states. The southern states were afraid that the north would push them into abandoning slavery on their sugar, tobacco and cotton plantations. So a very brutish civil war broke out in 1861, and did not end until 1865. The north triumphed and slavery became technically a thing of the past.

The cricket crunch

But what of cricket? In the thick of war, pitches were either ploughed up for food crops or trampled by troops. Soldiers on the march took up a quicker game that could be fitted in between battles. It was based on that fast fun sport, rounders. Yes, it was baseball, which towards the end of the 19th century surged ahead as the American nation's favourite game. It was one that did not remind them that Britain once ruled America.

Cricket limped on until the 1920s. But trees soon grew over the cricket pitches once dotted around New York's Central Park. Nevertheless, a few stoic clubs remained. And one of these was the fabulous Philadelphia, which clung on until the 1920s. Its second ground still survives, but is the venue for homegrown sports.

What now in the Americas?

The very first full-grown cricket stadium in the United States was completed in April, 2008 and was graced with its first match in May. Located at Fort Lauderdale, Florida, the sunshine capital, the venue should in time produce some fine, fast cricket. Will the pitch become a treat for fast bowlers? A magnet for the big hitters? Who knows? That depends on the ground staff, who will craft a whole new, unique character on that living, breathing patch of earth.

In the hubbub of New York, Eric Goldstein from the education department was really impressed when he noticed some young cricketers playing the game in parks, all dressed up in their smart whites. So in 2008 he pushed for a Middle School League, which involved 650 students and 14 teams. The seeds are sown. Let's hope they sprout into another cricketing nation.

West Indies

From the 17th century, several million Africans were transported to the Americas, subjected to forced labour and brutalised. The sole purpose for their slavery was to grow sugar and tobacco for the Empire. There is absolutely no good reason why they should want to play the game of their oppressors. Yet the Caribbean islanders did play. They played it brilliantly, too, triumphing countless times over the colonialists. Island pride kept local competition keen. Together, as the West Indies, the best of the islands' players proved formidable.

The West Indies entered the ICC (International Cricket Council) at an early stage, in 1926. Since then, the rollcall of cricket greats has seemed endless: Learie Constantine, Garfield Sobers, Malcolm Macdonald, Courtney Walsh, Curtley Ambrose and Brian Lara. Class batsmen, devastating fast bowlers and relentless all-rounders.

And many expatriates living in the United States are helping to galvanise the game, like the East Canje team in New York. This injection of deep tradition and skills is known as 'nostalgia' cricket. And while we are on the subject of nostalgia, what happened to cricket in India — Britain's 'jewel in the crown'?

Jhulan Goswami of India — 2007 women's ICC Player of the Year. See page 101 for more on Jhulan.

6 India — the jewel in the cricket CROWN

With a game like gilli-danda embedded in the genes and the culture, cricket was a mere step — not a stride — for sportsmen of the Indian subcontinent. Batting, bowling, fielding, and appealing were already part of their game, which just needed tweaking. All the British did was what they knew best, and that was organise. So cricket clubs were organised and the skills and aims of gilli-danda slipped effortlessly into a new form.

But how did the British get there and why? From the 17th century Britain viewed the Indian subcontinent as a goldmine or, more accurately, a jewel mine. More than this, Britain saw it as a way to control trade from the Far East to the West. By 1613 the British had blasted Portuguese traders out of the waters just off the west coast of India near the port of Surat.

From Surat, Britain's East India Company set her sights on the east coast, to control the Far East trade in silks and spices. The bold, aggressively expanding Company set up ports, trading forts and cricket clubs in very well positioned parts of the coast — Kolkata, Chennai,

Mumbai — now flourishing cricketing cities. And very soon, in 1721, the first record of a cricket match was made.

Local talent, local control

There was a whole harvest of local Indian cricket talent just waiting to be reaped. The British, however, couldn't bring themselves to let Indians join their clubs. But the Parsee community of Mumbai didn't hang around. In 1848 they set up their own club — the 'Oriental Club'. It was restricted to members of the Parsee faith, but was the seedbed of local cricket development.

The British finally challenged the Oriental Club to a match in 1877. This event helped galvanise other local cricketers into action. From 1912 the Parsee, Hindu and Muslim communities of Mumbai took part in a four-way tournament with the British. From these, a national Indian team began to tour. By 1926, India was accepted into the ICC, and played its first match against England in 1932 led by C.K. Nayudu.

These days, India is a hothouse of talent, the hub of cricket sponsorship, and an innovator in the game. The blockbuster Indian Players' League in 2008 came hot on the heels of the Indian Cricket League, which began in 2007. These fast 20-over, half-day games are bringing new spectators and grassroots enthusiasm for the game. The multiplex of cricket has hit the old order.

And the old order is holding up very nicely. With its endless rollcall of superbats such as Sachin Tendulkar and Virender Sehwag, India has achieved consistent top marks. In October 2010, India defeated Australia in a

Test series for the second time in a row. This back-to-back victory was followed by a series draw against South Africa — great results that led to India's number one spot in the Test Rankings. The icing on the cake was winning the 2011 World Cup One Day International (ODI) trophy on home soil.

Australia still held the top ODI Ranking, but with India chasing their tail, who knows for how long? And if India's opponents think that once the likes of Tendulkar and Sehwag have retired, then India will be toppled then they will be sorely disappointed. Rohit Sharma, Virat Kohl, Suresh Raina are just a few of the top young batsmen waiting hungrily — and practising — in the wings.

My country, my cricket

One of the strangest things about being part of the British Empire was the division of loyalty. Were you Indian or British? Or Indian and British? In those early days of international cricket, K.S. Ranjitsinhji decided that he was indeed both. He served his country, India, as a member of the royal family of Nawanagar. And he represented England, the colonial invader, at cricket. At the time, most people would not have batted an eyelid at this double loyalty.

Colonel His Highness Sri Sir Ranjitsinhji Vibhaji, Maharaja Kumar Jam Sahib of Nawanagar (1872–1933)

There are some cricketers who stand out among the crowd. K. S.

Ranjitsinjhi, or 'Ranji' was one of them.

This Indian Royal was among the most regal batsman ever seen. His strokes had touch and lightness, strength and movement all at once. Some said that they looked like conjuring tricks. He was one of the first batsmen to understand the impact of flexible footwork on placing the ball. It enabled him to carve strokes out of once seemingly impossible deliveries. He was a master against spin bowling — he could read it like a book.

His classic 'new look' style saw him move back, with weight on the back foot, then across to meet the ball, and always with his head forward. This gave him balance, space and great control to time the stroke. He could pivot and guide the ball to surprising parts of the ground. No one had seen anything like it before, and in England the crowds flocked just to catch a glimpse of this sensational player.

But England was at first a hostile host for the Prince. In his first three years at Cambridge University his talent and enthusiasm for the game were snubbed. In the fourth, Ranji finally bagged his Cambridge 'blue' — an award earned by students at the highest level of sporting competition. From there on he served his county, Sussex, with skill, loyalty and tremendous hard work. By 1900 he had twice scored 3,000 runs in a season. And for England, he delighted the crowds at Manchester's Old Trafford ground with 62 in the first innings and 154 not out in the second. In 1897/98 in Sydney, he carved an amazing 175 in his first Test against Australia.

When the cricket season was over, Ranji transformed into a prince. He joined the English upper classes in shooting parties, then returned to India to catch up with royal things. At the beginning of World War I, Ranji gathered together Indian soldiers to fight for Britain, the country that had suppressed them for so long. He fought in the war between 1914 and 1915, and survived to represent India at the new League of Nations. He finally succeeded to his throne and became the first top-class batting Maharaja of Nawanagar.

We can see the legacy of the great Ranjitsinjhi in colossal batsmen like Mohammed Azharuddin and Sashen Tendulkar in their stance, preparation, footwork, timing, ball placement and endless gracefulness.

Ranji's rod

Cricket, like life, is a game that has brought out the best and the worst in people. Ranjhitsinhji moved patiently past the first snubs from Cambridge University and became an international star. But this did not protect him from the rod of further racism. Most notably from his one-time closest friend, the outstanding cricketing all-rounder and intellectual, C.B. Fry. Later, though, Fry became bombastic and crazed, and in the 1920s followed the poisoned path laid by Adolph Hitler. This is neither the first nor last incident of racism in cricket. And it not only came from players but also crowds, umpires and selection panels.

7 Cricket rises from a divided NATION

India gained independence from British rule in 1947. Immediately, religious ties that had shaped early cricket clubs became deep social divisions. Violent civil strife split the nation. Millions were killed or displaced as Muslims clustered in the north-east and north-west of the country, and Hindus to the rest.

Out of the chaos came two countries, India and Pakistan. And from these two cricketing nations came two distinct styles. We are now blessed with an India that stuns with classic, stylish batting and intelligent, mesmerising spin bowling. And a Pakistan that thrills with punishing pace and a seemingly endless stream of attacking all-rounders.

Pakistan — no pushover

This new Pakistan team hit the international scene in the 1952/3 season, when it faced a confident, stylish India. Known as 'the babes of international cricket', Pakistan equipped themselves well, losing only two matches to one. Three other tight contests were a draw. Pakistan could hold its own.

Abdul Hafeez Kardar, had been part of the Indian side

that played England in 1946. He had played for Oxford University, and the Warwickshire county championship team. If anyone was in any doubt about the benefit of playing club and first team cricket abroad, then Captain Kardar was the man to prove it unfounded. But then, this internationality had grown from a culture of dual belongings. Like Ranjitsinhji before him, his skill and cricket brain were nurtured in two countries — Pakistan and England. He had captained a winning Indian side against England's MCC in 1945.

But in 1954 his new side, Pakistan, had to face an England with some formidable bowlers, like Brian Statham, Alec Bedser and Bob Appleyard. They also had to face a rain-soaked British summer. By the last game at south London's Kennington Oval, Pakistan had dripped their way to one dreadful loss and two draws. But at the Oval, magic often happens. The little ground lifts your spirits with the cheering chirps of south Londoners and it certainly worked for Pakistan. For here they proved their place in cricket's world order. It was the shape of things to come. Young Fazal Mahmud dazzled the batsmen with his smooth pace and bewitching pitch of the ball. He took Captain Len Hutton's team by the throat, and 12 wickets for a knockout 99 runs. English newspapers splashed the only fitting headline: 'England Fazzaled!'

In 1956, Pakistan beat Australia in Karachi. A momentous moment for them and especially Fazal Mahmud, who took 13 wickets for 114 runs. Pakistan as a cricketing nation had truly arrived. With top-class all-rounders like Imran

Khan, and fearsome fast bowlers in Waqar Younis and Wasim Akram, Pakistan were a force to be reckoned with in the 1990s.

With talent in all spheres of the game, it is difficult to believe that in 2011 Pakistan lay sixth in both the Test and One Day International Rankings. Their results can be brilliant — in 2009 they won the ICC Twenty20 World Cup trophy. They played a cracking semi-final match in the 2011 World Cup against India, losing but entertaining the deafening crowd.

Players can seem to be many things. They can seem to be unruly — the 2010 season saw allegations and prosecutions for match fixing. Players can seem to be passionate — nothing wrong with that! And they can seem a bit stroppy, too. In 2011, leading batsman Shahid Afridi criticised coach and cricket legend Waqar Younis for his team selection. Surprisingly, this was during a 3-2 win against the West Indies! But with all their flair and their fire, who would be without Pakistan? Well, possibly Bangladesh...

The birth of Bangladesh

The Indian subcontinent was still unsettled as each country shuffled uncomfortably in its new shoes. Pakistan was united by the religion of Islam. But the lands of East and West Pakistan were divided by a massive 1,600 km slab of India. Their peoples were divided by differences in language and culture. So in 1971, after more conflict, they parted. West Pakistan became just Pakistan. East Pakistan was reborn as Bangladesh.

It took only a year to establish the Bangladesh Cricket

Control Board, and cricket leagues in Dhaka and Chittagong. From then on, cricket exploded. In 1977, Bangladesh became an associate member of the ICC and only 20 years later gained the right to take part in One Day Internationals against the top-flight teams. The year 2000 saw Bangladesh enter the Test match arena. The nation's instinct to get 'em while they're young has borne fruit. Many other, more powerful, cricketing nations could learn from the this new kid on the block.

Even so, Bangladesh's take off into the Test arena has hit some storms. In 2005 they toured England and were hammered, losing by an innings each time. This roasting 'inspired' commentators Mike Atherton and Richie Benaud to question Bangladesh's rise into the Test ranks. Weren't they missing the point , as many pundits do, that new Test sides need to play top teams again and again to strengthen their cricket and match-play skills.

Disaster struck in September 2008 when 13 members of the Bangladesh team were banned from international cricket for 10 whole years for joining the Indian Cricket League. The big bucks and bright lights were just too much temptation for the players. A whole new generation of Bangladesh cricketers had to step up to the plate.

And they did. When New Zealand toured Bangladesh in 2010, the home team won four out of the five One Day Internationals (ODI). The fifth was abandoned due to bad weather. But in 2011, Bangladesh lost every single match in the World Cup ODI, hosted in India, Sri Lanka and, poignantly, Bangladesh. Such is the roller-coaster ride of cricket.

Mohammad Rafique (1970–)

Rafique is a household name in Bangladesh and he is one of the few Bangladeshi players to appear in the ICC's top 50 for bowler rankings.

Rafique began his career with Bangladesh Sporting at the age of 15 and at 18 he joined the Bangladesh Biman cricket team. A handy low-order batsman, Rafique's claim to fame is his bowling which is a slow left-arm orthodox style. The bowler was better known for his performance in the One-Day International (ODI) games, but he also played Test cricket and joined the Indian Cricket League (ICL) in 2000, which saw him banned by the Bangladesh Cricket Board for ten years from all forms of cricket.

Sri Lankan fielder, Aravinda da Silva, right, attempts to catch the ball off the bat of South African, Makhaya Ntini.

8 Sri Lanka — small BUT MIGHTY!

Like a pearl drop on a gold earring, the island of Sri Lanka dangles south of the mighty Indian subcontinent. But her cracking, classy cricket history began when she had another name — Ceylon. Ceylon was famed for her tea and wherever there is tea, there's an Englishman. In fact, lots of them, which is the main reason why cricket eventually came to Ceylon. Although if it hadn't been for just one man, the island might have escaped England's attention.

Robert Knox (1641–1720)

Robert Knox was an Englishman who may have played the first game of cricket in Ceylon, but we will never know for sure whether he did or not. What we do know is that he brought a lot of Englishmen to Ceylon who *did* bring the great game to this beautiful island. And this is how it happened.

Robert Knox's father, also Robert Knox, was an English sea captain in the service of the British East Africa Company. In 1659, young Robert spent some time with his father at the north-east Indian trading port of St George Fort, now Chennai. After finishing company business there, Robert, his father and other Company men set sail for home. They had to sail right down the east coast, around the bottom of India and then westward back to England. But fair weather turned foul just as they reached the island of Ceylon. A wild, wet wind rammed their vessel ashore in the Bay of Trincomalee.

The 19 exhausted survivors, including the two Knox men, dragged themselves onto the sands. They were delighted when they saw some locals running towards them in the distance. But they were less than delighted when the locals cried, 'We capture you in the name of the King of Kandy!'

The so-called 'captives' were treated like no others, for the kind King of Kandy allowed them the freedom of the island. Over the next 19 years, they settled and married local women, had children and generally became part of the island community. Robert Knox's father sadly died of malaria, but young Robert survived by dealing in rice, corn and other goods. After nineteen years he and another survivor decided that it was time to go home, so they escaped to a Dutch settlement on the north-west of the island. From there, they sailed back to England.

Robert became a sea captain in the British East India Company, just like his father. But he never forgot Ceylon, and encouraged British interest there. By 1785 the Britons had ousted both Dutch and Portuguese traders, and set up plantations of rubber, indigo, sugar, coffee and, of course, tea. The noble Kingdom of Kandy stubbornly held onto the east of the island, but fell to the British in 1815. The British brought with them their sports and pastimes, and a new piece of cricket history was about to be made.

Goodbye Ceylon, hello Sri Lanka

Cricket caught hold in the 19th century in Ceylon. As well as English interest, migrant workers from Malaya boosted Sri Lankan cricket with the game they'd been taught by English traders back in Indonesia. They set up their own Colombo Malay Club in 1872 and added to the cricket mix.

By 1926 a national Ceylon side played its opening first-class match against an MCC team. It took place at the capital city Colombo's graceful, tree-lined Nomads Ground at Victoria Park. Although Ceylon lost by an innings, they continued to develop their game and structure until they gained Test status in 1981. By this time, the islanders had shaken off the colonial name of Ceylon (in 1972) and changed it to Sri Lanka.

Sri Lanka came into its own in the 1990s, and — with the stylish batting of Sanath Jayasuriya and Aravinda da Silva — became a formidable one-day side, winning the World Cup in 1996 and becoming runners-up in 2007 and 2011, and reaching the semi-finals in 2010. Their Twenty20 runner's up title in 2009 gave warning that Sri Lanka in this new format would be a force to reckon with.

Among the talented players that have made this possible, one stands out — world-class spin bowler, Muttiah Muralitharan, who stars later in this book. Since his retirement in 2011, Sri Lanka are having to rethink their bowling line-up. But they have talented batsmen like Tillakaratne Dilshan and Tharanga Paranavitana to notch up good scores and take the pressure off their less experienced bowlers.

Indigenous Australian men in cricket team, 1868.

9 Brave new WORLD

It was all America's fault. The Americans could no longer put up with the enormous taxes imposed on them by their British masters so they claimed their independence in 1784. This meant that Britain had nowhere to send her petty criminals. Never mind. Their decision to ship them out to Australia meant that the Great Game had an opportunity to grow in a great land.

As early as 1788, the first English convict ship rocked and rolled into Botany Bay. The future of the game did not look bright, for the 700 largely petty criminals had landed in a hot, sticky swamp. Certainly not good for the fast bowling that Australia is renowned for now. With no fresh water to be found, the fleet moved north to a cove with a beautiful forest and a trickling stream. This became Sydney Harbour — gateway to New South Wales and one of the most successful cricketing states anywhere in the world.

Britain had designs on Australia and many politicians saw beyond its role as a penal colony. Some felt it would make a tidy trading post. Others, a plantation for flax and naval timbers to help keep Britain afloat (or perhaps to make cricket bats with). Whatever the plans, the colony needed a lot of man and woman power. So, by 1793 the first free settlers arrived in Australia. And the rest is cricketing history.

The duel begins

Australia was first represented abroad with the Australian Aboriginal cricket team tour of England in 1868. It took the tourists 79 days to get there, followed by a gruelling schedule that took in 40 grounds across the island and entered into the cricket consciousness of two nations. In 1877, the English side clashed with a different Australian team, striking up a magnetic sporting relationship at the MCG in Melbourne. Although it wasn't called a Test match then, it is certainly recognised as one now.

From then on, the contest heated up. The Sydney riots of 1879 just about summed up the growing tension between England and Australia. They erupted during a match at what is now known as the Sydney Cricket Ground between the English tourists, captained and organised by Lord Harris, and a team from the New South Wales Cricket Association, led by Dave Gregory. The riots surrounded slurs printed in the *Sydney Morning Herald* concerning umpiring disputes, match fixing and inappropriate betting amongst match officials. Pressure mounted when Australia toured England in 1882.

The Australian XI, 1880.

Ashes clashes

> *'In affectionate remembrance of English cricket, which died at the Oval on 29th August 1882. Deeply lamented by a large circle of sorrowing friends. R.I.P. N.B. The body will be cremated and the ashes taken to Australia.'*
> — THE SPORTING TIMES, 1882, ON ENGLAND'S DEFEAT AT HOME TO AUSTRALIA.

It was never called the Ashes to start with. It wasn't even called a Test. But it was one of the most important episodes in the development of international cricket. It really began in 1880, when England won the series. So in 1882, the Australian team was looking for revenge.

The pivotal match was held at the atmospheric Kennington Oval in south London. William Lloyd Murdoch's Australian side was doing really badly, reaching a total of only 63 in the first innings. But with the genius of Fred 'Demon' Spofforth, who took 14 wickets for 90 runs, Australia won. And this is what inspired the above obituary for the 'death' of English cricket.

England's next tour to Australia was led by the Honourable Ivo Bligh, who, perhaps jokingly, referred to the 'Ashes' while in Adelaide. Moving on to Melbourne, he was invited to a Christmas party and a casual game of cricket at 'Rupertswood'. This was the home of the cricket legend, William Clarke. Again, Ivo referred to the 'Ashes' taunt. Later, a group of ladies presented Ivo with a little urn, which is thought to contain the ashes of cricket equipment — possibly a bail, ball or stump — used during that casual Christmas match.

And that would have probably been the end of it. But Ivo Bligh had taken a fancy to one of the lovely ladies who so kindly gave him the urn, all wrapped up in a hand-sewn velvet bag. She was Florence Murphy, who, with little hesitation said 'Oh, yes!' when Ivo asked her to marry him.

The *Melbourne Punch* printed a poem to them both — it was of course about the Ashes. And the tussle between the two nations has never looked back. As for Ivo Bligh, he returned to England with his bride, and later became the Eighth Earl of Darnely. After his death, Florence donated the urn to the MCC, where it still sits.

Out of all the Ashes series, Australia has risen like the phoenix that she is, winning 38 times to England's 28. Five tests have been drawn.

Should Australia retain the actual urn every time she wins? Or should England have to keep it as a sore reminder of her inadequacies? These questions are continually debated.

Billy Murdoch (Australia, 1854–1911)

Billy Murdoch was a brilliant batsman at a time when bowlers still held the advantage. He courted controversy twice, by his involvement in the Sydney riots and in the players' strike over their share of gate money. He was also a trailblazer. He settled in England, and, with John Ferris, was the first to have played for two nations.

Forging ahead

Australian cricketers knew that there was a great wide world of cricket opportunities just waiting for them. But they needed to be organised. So in 1892, New South Wales, South Australia and Victoria formed the Australian Cricket Council to administer the game. It only lasted until 1898. But in 1905, the new Australian Board of Control for International Cricket was formed. And this actually began to fund its international team, paving the way for a strong side. The ABCIC is now known as Cricket Australia.

Warwick Windridge Armstrong (Australia,1879–1947)

Known as The Big Ship, all-rounder Warwick Armstrong began his career as a willowy young chap. With his baggy, billowing trousers and his baggy green Australian cap he began his cricketing career lean, hungry and mean. But by his late 20s, the six-foot (1.8 m) Armstrong was simply enormous, adding power to his game that was at that time unmatched. The Big Ship's batting was ferocious, especially on the leg side. As a bowler, his fast medium leg-break ball deceived in flight, which frightened batsmen into very defensive play. And Armstrong encouraged this by setting his field close to catch any nicks from a nervous shot — a sign of his skills as an intelligent tactician.

Captain Armstrong liked to rest his attacking bowlers to keep them fresh for the next battle when he knew a match was leading to a draw. Then he'd take himself off to the outfield, where he'd calmly read a newspaper dropped by a spectator. Armstrong has been unfairly judged for unsportsmanlike tactics on the pitch, but fairly criticised for his acid attacks on cricket teams and players when he turned to journalism after retirement.

Between 1898 and 1922, Armstrong played 50 Test matches and scored 45 centuries in first-class cricket. His Sheffield Shield tally totalled a staggering 4993 matches, averaging 49.93 runs. And he took 832 wickets for 19.71 runs apiece.

Gathering in the game

By the end of the 19th century it was clear that Australia, England and South Africa were the big cheeses of cricket. So in 1909, the Australian and South African cricket presidents swaggered off to Lord's where the Earl of Chesterfield, President of the MCC, hosted a meeting. The outcome was pivotal to the development of cricket, for the three nations created the Imperial Cricket Conference (ICC, which today stands for International Cricket Council) — an organisation that would lay down rules for 'international' competition. But notice the word 'Imperial'. It meant that membership included only those nations within the British Empire.

So while cricket did not disappear in Europe or America, it was sidelined. And for many decades no one in the ICC really bothered whether those outside the Commonwealth played it or not. Cricket development and expansion was low on the horizon. Nevertheless, the ICC shaped and firmed up the international scene. Each of the three nations called its national team a 'Test' side. By 1929 they were ready to accept three other members and Test sides: the West Indies, India and New Zealand — still all countries within the Empire at the time. Pakistan, a new nation in 1948, became a full member of the ICC in 1953. Sri Lanka and Bangladesh have joined since, while Kenya is still knocking at their door.

Today, the ICC is keen to encourage cricket everywhere in the world and to support it financially wherever it can. Its 33 associate members include some very hot sides, like Canada and the Netherlands, while the 58 affiliate members belong to nations as diverse as Peru and Afghanistan.

ICC — always in a crisis?

But all has not been plain sailing for the ICC. There have been some huge political decisions. Like barring South Africa in 1968 for its Apartheid politics — politics that did not allow Africans to share the same parts of the beach, bus or ballpark, never mind the all-white national cricket team.

There have been criticisms, too, over its policies towards umpires. In 2008, Australian cricketers felt uneasy about the ICC's governance. Two-thirds thought it a dangerous precedent when the ICC stood down umpire Steve Bucknor ahead of the Perth Test against India. It followed decisions that Bucknor made during the 2007/08 Sydney Test. Would this weaken the role of the umpire?

Whatever the arguments about the ICC, they do uphold the laws first made by the MCC over 200 years ago. Rules that have carried the game through many changes in shape and length.

10 And it's time FOR TEA

Cricket is full of quaint customs, like the tea break. Like the Twelfth Man 'bringing on the drinks' — the old-fashioned summer kind of drinks, like orange and lemon squash. So here is your tea break from cricket history. A short romp through the rules, which will hopefully take you through to the history of how the game is played, and perhaps encourage you to pick up the bat yourself...

Rough rules

This is basically how you'd play the game on a proper pitch. But if you want to play it in a park or backyard with a tennis ball and a stick, that's okay too. The rules are simple for now. But as with most worthwhile things, the devil's in the detail. You'll find plenty of details later on. For now, the main idea is that there are two teams. Each team tries to hit the ball as well as they can. They score as many runs as possible without losing their best batsmen to great bowlers and sharp fielders.

But the most important thing of all is to create a team and to play regularly. You will then find that cricket characters emerge. Nicknames get bandied about, and funny little foibles develop. A history grows. And with it stories to tell your children and grandchildren until they weep with weariness.

Cricket recipe

Ingredients

1 You will need 22 people, eleven players for each team, with two 'extras', each known as the 'Twelfth Man'. You might have to persuade the extras to come along as often they don't get much to do. Although occasionally they help win the match with a classy catch.

2 A grassy field cut fairly short. It needs a rectangular patch somewhere near the middle. The patch is actually called a pitch and is often made of yellowing grass stubble rather than blades. The pitch is 22 yards long (20.12 m), which is called a 'chain'.

3 A hard leather-covered ball, usually red. Its circumference must measure between 224 and 229 cm.

4 Two broad sticks with thinner handles, called bats.

5 Two 'wickets', one at each end of the pitch. Each wicket is made of three long sticks, each 28 inches (71.1 cm) tall. Two short sticks called bails nestle in grooves at the top. The sticks are pushed into the ground to a total width of 9 inches (22.86 cm). They stand straight and parallel to each other.

6 There are a lot of 22s in cricket, as you can see — '22' could be an omen. Omens, suspicions, lucky charms,

these are all part of cricket. These could be ingredients too. Choose your own charm before you play.

Method

1 One team of 11 players takes to the field with the ball to bowl and field. Get them to take their places at various points around the cricket ground.

2 Take two of the other team and give them each a bat. Leave the others to watch behind the boundary. These spectators must concentrate very hard on the game and not mess about. This is because they will each have to go and bat when one of their team members is 'out'. They must be ready and padded up as their turn nears. Sharing bats is okay. So is sharing pads.

3 One batsman must stand at the striker's end, the end where the batsman is going to strike the ball. The other stands at the opposite wicket, at the bowler's end.

4 A bowler from the other team runs towards the batsman and bowls the ball. But the bowler must not step on or over the bowler's 'popping crease' as he bowls. This 'crease' is a line in front of the bowler's wicket.

5 The batsman judges if the ball is easy to hit without getting out. If the batsman hits the ball out of the reach of the fielders, then both batsmen must try to score a run by scampering to the opposite wicket. They should run as many times as they can, passing each other as they go. And they should keep count of the score of these runs. This is vital.

6 The batsmen must yell 'Stay!' — or something similar — if the fielders look as if they're going to get hold of the ball.

7 The bowler and the fielding team must try to get the batsmen 'out' in one of four main ways:
   - The bowler hits the wicket with the ball.
   - The batsman finds the bowler's ball so difficult to hit that he puts his leg or another part of his body in front of the wicket to stop the ball hitting it. This is called 'leg before wicket', or 'LBW'.
   - Fielders catch the ball when the batsman hits it in the air without it bouncing first.
   - Fielders hit a wicket with the ball before the batsman reaches the crease.

8 Keep going until all the batsmen are out. Try to change the bowler occasionally as it is very tiring work. The fielders should move around too. Then they'll be in the best position to catch or stop the ball when it's hit. When the batsmen are all out, swap the teams so that the batting team bowls and fields. The other team bats to get as many runs as possible while the fielding team tries to get them out.

9 When the teams have finished batting, then they've each completed an innings. You can count up the number of runs each has made and see which team has won. Or you could do it all again.

10 Bake all of the above in Earth's oven at a variety of temperatures for several hours, or even days. Weeks if it's a tournament with lots of different teams.

Bending the rules

Cricket can really be played anywhere, with any number of people and quite a few rule changes. It is a game to be enjoyed, even on ice! An international ice cricket tournament has been played since 1988 on Lake St Moritz in Switzerland. But real ice cricket was created in 2001 by Jason Barry, the coach of the Estonia National Cricket Team.

Teams can have between 6 and 10 players and every team bowls six overs. Wides count as two extra runs, which seems a bit tough as the bowler must skid around a lot. If a batsman hits a skater, a cross-country skier or a moose, he gets six extra runs. Now there's something to aim for!

This is a whole, cold world away from a perfect cricket pitch.

Test match, England v. Australia at Lord's Cricket Ground, 1945.

11 Perfect PITCH

The cricket pitch is a sacred rectangle of earth and grass. At times, it appears like a patch of stubble and as if a dog-fight has gouged the creases at either end. But make no mistake; the pitch is truly a wizard's spell. Only the groundsman is allowed to touch it: to maintain the character of the place; to keep it a slow 'wicket' or fast or flat or turning. Or maybe, just for a season or two, to whip up controversy and flip its character right over to surprise a touring team.

Grass of the past

In 1744 the first Laws of Cricket stated that the length of the cricket pitch was to be 22 yards (20.12 m). It still is that length (20.12 m). But until the 19th century it was still quite a rough affair. Even the pitch at Lord's was clipped with hand scythes and grazing sheep. At that time, most wickets were a true bowler's paradise, with uneven grass, and peaks and troughs just lurking to spin the ball off in all directions. Batsmen had little chance of a high score.

In those days, as now, cricketers understood how sensitive the ball was to changes on the ground. Slight morning dew, and the ball could skid; hot midday sun, and the ball could spin in the dust or jerk on a crack. Things would improve slightly if only there was a way of cutting the grass finer. And during the great 18th century age of innovation, this is exactly what happened.

In 1830, Edwin Beard Budding created a lawnmower based on a carpet cutter that he had seen in a factory. This new machine not only mowed grass but also rolled it. Budding took out a patent for his machine in 1832, and the design has altered little since. This farsighted inventor described his lawnmower as:

> '...a new combination and application of machinery for the purpose of cropping or shearing the vegetable surfaces of lawns, grass-plants and pleasure grounds.'

Just perfect for cricket pitches. All the lawnmower needed now was a motor to take away some of the hard work in the massive outfield. And in 1893, James Summer obliged with the first steam-powered lawnmower.

Growing a pitch

But there is a lot more to keeping a perfect pitch than just cutting it. The strip of turf has a construction a bit like an ancient Roman road. Soil is dug out down to about 300 mm and is then filled with a layer of crushed stone, gravel, soil and topsoil. Special grass is planted and plastic sheeting tucked down along the sides of the pitch to prevent rogue grasses from growing through from the rest of the ground. This pampered patch is then lovingly fertilised, mowed, rolled, swept and in-filled. But pitches, like all other cricket matters, are subject to rules policed by the ICC. No repair work can be carried out while a match is in progress. No sneaking out in the middle of the night to replace divots or scuff the pitch up a bit. New Zealand groundsmen got rapped over the knuckles for one such incident in March 2004, during a Test against South Africa. 'Pitch tampering' just isn't cricket, even if it seems innocent enough.

No one except the groundsman is allowed to prod or poke a pitch, either. Just ask Geoffrey Boycott, one-time England opening batsman. He stuck a key into the cracks of a wicket at Lord's and was politely asked to step back. Boycott was only seeing how dry it was so that he could report its condition for the cricket broadcast he was making. Innocent enough again, but against the Laws of Cricket.

PITCH POINTS

- Most large cricket grounds have up to five wickets to play on. They run parallel to each other and together are called 'the square'. The pitches are not necessarily all used in the same season.
- A batting side can ask for the roller — either heavy or light. But are they just clutching at straws? On a dry pitch, a heavy rolling compacts the ground for about an hour. But then the snags and crags seem to pop up again. A light roller just smooths over the surface and crunches up those little pips of dirt. On a damp pitch, a light roller achieves little, while a heavy one calms the pitch into a firm slab. But it's all a matter

of taste and tactics.

- In 1934, Essex first class county cricket returned to the Brentwood ground. There were murmurings that the pitch just wouldn't be right. But no worries, the groundsman spread a good bucketful of liquid cow manure on it. Perhaps there wasn't too much diving to save runs on the first day's play.

Problems with pitches

Every ground has two distinct ends. Each has a different aspect, slope, prevailing wind direction — and a different history. The MCC's Lord's Ground in London has a Pavilion End and a Nursery End. Players often liked to warm up behind the Nursery End stand, where pineapples once grew in Henderson's Nursery hothouses. That was until the 1880s when Lords bought the land. This end is all right outside the grounds. But inside it is at the bottom end of an eight-foot (2.4 m) slope that rises towards Lord's Pavilion. A captain has to choose his bowlers very carefully to make sure that they can either climb the slope or control the ball and themselves going down the other way!

But whatever the pitch — be it the finest grass or coir matting over a piece of concrete — bowlers will always try to make the most of it.

PLAYER POSITIONS

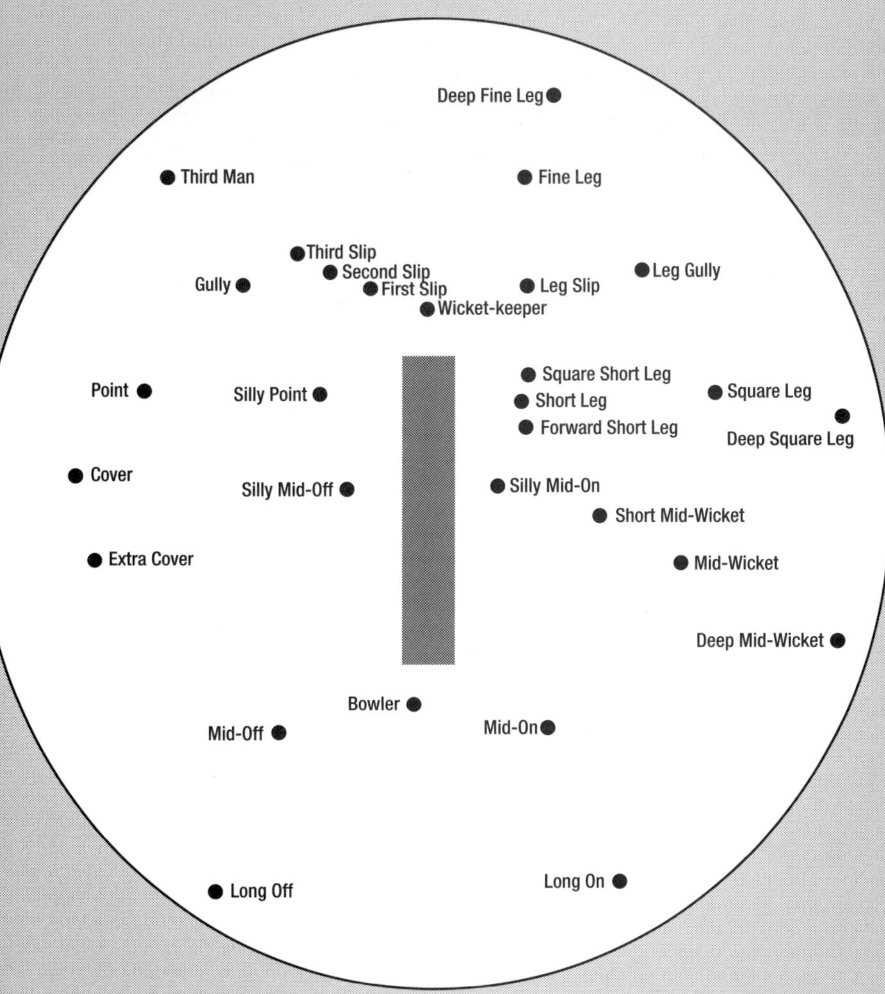

1932/33 Australia v. England Bodyline Series. W.M. Woodfull ducks under a rising ball from Larwood. D.R. Jardine, the England captain, is at the left of the infield cordon.

12 Bowled OVER

'Down the mine I dreamed of cricket. I bowled imaginary balls in the dark. I sent the stumps spinning and heard them rattling in the tunnels.'

HAROLD LARWOOD, ENGLAND FAST BOWLER (1904–1995), ONCE A PIT LAD DOWN THE MINE, WHO BOWLED IN THE ONLY SHOES HE COULD AFFORD — SANDSHOES.

A lot of balls

In ancient times, bowlers used stones, rolled-up sheep's wool, birds' quills and even a block of cheese. The only thing in common with today's cricket ball is that none of them had great bounce. Things improved with cork, which does bounce quite a lot.

The first six-seam ball was made by Dukes of Penshurst in Kent in 1780. They probably didn't realise that the seam would become as important as the ball itself in bamboozling the batsman. A seam bounced straight on a grassy pitch will create friction and the ball spins off at an angle, which makes it hard for the batsman to read.

These days, the ball isn't just leather and stitches. The best is made from a hard core of rubber and cork (Portuguese cork's the best), then a dozen layers of cork and wool (some say New Zealand is prime, like their lamb, while others prefer English wool). The whole thing is encased in top-notch tanned leather and hand-sewn with thread made of six twisted fibres. A good wax and polish — or even a dose of nitrocellulose lacquer — and it's ready. Quality.

And this is how the bowler uses the cherry to pip his man.

Flippers, floaters and other bowling terms

Is it a sport, a skill, a science or an art? It is perhaps all of these, and it also needs a big helping of psychology and a lot of stamina. A bowler has to read the player, pitch, slope, wind and moisture in the air. He has to be aware of what stage the game is at, what tactics to employ and where the fielders are placed.

Then he looks at the ball. Is it getting a bit old? Does he need to shine it on one side just a smidgeon more to get some spin? Is the seam a bit scuffed? When he's weighed up all these choices, he can find his run-up mark and begin. He might be fast, slow, or medium-paced. He might turn the ball or aim straight for the block. Whatever his style, he'll be thirsting for that next wicket. Here's some of the types of bowlers and the ways they torture batsmen. The bowlers and deliveries in the list are aiming at a right-handed batsman.

Arm ball Cunning little chap, this one. The batsman faces the off-spinner thinking the ball's going to spin from left to right. But the bowler's holding the ball so that the seam is straight — that means it's vertical. Then he turns the ball with just his forefinger, so there is no spin on it, and the ball just goes sailing straight towards the stumps.

Banana-bender You won't even see this coming. It's a 144 kph ball with a swerve on it. Pakistan's Waqar Younis made this his own in the 1990s.

Bouncer Every fast bowler wants to get the batsman out first ball. What could be better than a bouncer that aims high onto the body? In first-class matches a bowler is allowed only two of these in each over.

Chinaman It's a left-arm wrist-spin ball that seems impossible, as it goes from the front of the hand as normal. But then it pitches to the left and turns into the right. Was it brought to the game by the West Indian, Ellis Achong, who was of Chinese descent? We don't really know. Another West Indian, the great all-rounder Sir Garfield St Auburn Sobers (1936–) bowled a devastating Chinaman. And that's without his two extra fingers that were removed at birth. He sent down a mean left swing ball, too.

Doosra It's an off-break ball with menace. Basically, it spins the other way from a normal off-break. The bowler bowls it from the back of his hand to get this effect, which is why some call this delivery a 'mystery ball', 'floater' or 'wrong-un'. Saqlain Mushtaq of Pakistan (1976–) who popularised the doosra has been developing another daring delivery called a Teesra.

Flipper Bowled more from the bottom of the hand, it glides sweetly in the air, then skids savagely along the ground.

Googly Basically, it's the leg-spinner's doosra. It's spun out of the back of the hand and moves from left to right. The batsman doesn't expect this from a leg-spinner. Australia's first googly specialist was Herbert V. Hordern (1883–1938). His bowling was so good he made batsmen really suspicious of his methods. During a Test series in Jamaica, he woke up one night with a start. At his bedside was a posse of West Indian cricketers trying to examine his arm while he slept, to see if it was bionic!

Leg-spinners Thought to be a dying art, Australian cricketer, Shane Warne, revived the leg-spinner's profile. Basically, the spinner uses his wrist and fingers to spin, and moves his shoulders to make the most of the spin. The ball is pitched right towards the leg side, then it moves to the left towards the stumps.

Off-spinners They use their fingers then some wrist to spin the ball from left to right off to leg. Muttiah Muralitharan of Sri Lanka (1972–) has made off-spin his own for over a decade. Muralitharan manages to get the ball to dip suddenly, utterly confusing the batsman.

Round-the-wicket Bowlers usually deliver (to a right-handed batsman, remember) with the umpire to their right. But occasionally they bowl on the other side, with the umpire to the left. It's more awkward to bowl, but the batsman finds the strange angle difficult to play. But it's hard to get an umpire to give a batsman out for LBW (leg before wicket) with a ball bowled round-the-wicket. The angle is usually too wide, or looks too wide.

Swinging yorker You think it won't be a yorker because it's not flying in a straight line. The next minute, it's straightened out and your stumps are clattering. Swing bowlers need moist, still air to curve the ball. They have a really hard time if the air's too dry and windy.

Topper A leg-spinner's dream if it goes well, this ball goes straight in the air, dips along the ground, and then skids. It's the first cousin of the flipper.

Yorker Fast bowlers love to plant this one at your feet, or even better, between your feet and the wicket. To 'york' someone in 19th-century speak meant to deceive them.

Zooter Shane Warne loves this delivery. The batsman thinks it's going to turn, and then it floats straight in.

13 Bowlers' PARADE

There have been some very special bowlers in the history of cricket. It is so hard to pick the best. Could it be Shane Warne with his sly deception and jaw-dropping inventiveness? Or lethal Lillee with his long, nerve-jangling approach and explosive delivery? A single great bowler can rarely do it alone. A captain has to use all his bowlers' talents to their optimum. He needs to understand the pitch and which bowlers will deliver best from each end. He will choose pairs that work well together — perhaps a seamer from one end and an off-spinner from the other, which will stop the batsman from getting too comfortable.

There are times when a team puts together a piece of bowling magic. Like India's spin quartet from the 1960s to the 1980s. No, not a dance group — for these particular four were far more entertaining. Bishen Bedi, E.A.S. Prasanna, Bhagawat Chandrasekhar and Srinivas Venkataraghavan — or Venkat as he was known — were four stunning spinners. They were rarely played in the same team, but in pairs they challenged batsmen in 225 Tests, taking over 800 wickets. Then there was the firepower of

Australia's Dennis Lillee and Jeff Thompson in the 1970s. Or West Indies' 1980s quartet: Joel Garner, Michael Holding, Andy Roberts and Malcolm Marshall, who *did* often play at the same time and with lethal results.

Spun gold and the Midas touch — the bowling of Warnie and Murali

Australia's Shane Warne is a bowling legend. Born in 1969, for over two decades he made as many headlines for his personal life as for his sumptuous spin. Sri Lanka's Muttiah Muralitharan is a bowling giant. Born in 1972, he has made as many headlines by the whingers who don't like his bowling action as he has for his dazzling doosra. These bowlers' careers, like their deliveries, have swung this way and that. So how do they stack up against each other?

Warne

2000 Chosen as number 4 in Wisden's Cricketer of the Century.

12 March 2004 Notches up his first 500 wickets.

October 2004 Warne betters Murali's Test match wickets taken.

2005 Warne takes 40 wickets against England for an average of 19.92 and he scores 249

Murali

1998 Takes his first ten-wicket haul against Zimbabwe in Sri Lanka's at the age of 26. Also takes 16 wickets for only 220 runs in the same year.

2002 Reaches ten 10-wicket hauls faster than any other bowler, including the great Richard Hadlee. In the same year Murali reaches his 400-wicket milestone in just 72 Tests — the fastest record ever.

runs as a lower-order batsman.

2006 Reaches the world record of 700 wickets at a Boxing Day Test match, exactly 15 years since his first Test and first wicket taken. It takes him 145 Tests to reach this milestone with an average of 25.41 runs per wicket.

2007 Shane retires from Test cricket after Australia thrashes England in the Ashes, 5-0.

1 June 2008 Coaches and captains the Rajasthan Royals, the first winning team of the new Indian Players' League Twenty20 tournament.

2011 Shane announces his retirement from Rajasthan Royals and the end of competitive cricket.

16 March 2004 Reaches his 500-wicket record, the fastest record for this feat and youngest bowler to do so.

May 2004 Murali beats Courtney Walsh's record of 519 Test match wickets.

2006 Murali is chosen as Wisden's Leading Cricketer in the World.

2007 Murali overtakes Warne's 700 wickets record. It takes him just 117 Tests and an average of only 21.47 runs. In the same year the ICC gives Murali a rating of 920 points, the highest ever for a spin bowler.

2010 Muralitharan's last Test match sees his 800th wicket — taken against India with the final ball of the match.

2011 Retires from One Day International cricket after the World Cup. Sri Lanka were runners-up. Murali a runner-up to no one — always at the top.

Australian bowling legend, Shane Warne.

Muttiah Muralitharan shows off his controversial bowling style.

Shane Warne would never have quipped that Muttiah Muralitharan was a straight-arm spinner, but some might have. For Murali's bowling action has been questioned down the years, especially in 2004 when umpire Darrell Hair continually 'no-balled' him for 'chucking' against Australia. Chucking means that you're straightening your arm again just as you're about to launch the ball. You can bowl with a slightly bent arm, but you must not then push it straight.

Murali has had biomechanical tests on his action in Perth, Australia, Hong Kong and England. Each test concentrated on his doosra. Murali's angle of delivery has been approved by the ICC, but the grumbles still continue, especially among disgruntled Australians. So let's give the last word to an Australian, former first-class batsman, Michael Slater, who attended the 2004 biomechanical test in England.

'In Australia there is an almost universal belief Muralitharan is a chucker. But if they were to see this footage they would be amazed. When people see this video, they say, "I've changed my mind, he's NOT a chucker."'

The ICC now allows a 15 degree straightening angle. This should please not only Muralitharan, but also other bowlers who have been accused of chucking in recent years, such as Brett Lee, Harbajhan Singh and Shoaib Malik. ICC tests led to another statement from them that rocked the cricket world: that 80 per cent of all bowlers straighten their arms beyond the legal limit. This statistic should quieten the whingers once and for all. As for Murali, he was born with an elbow that cannot extend properly. He bowls superbly with this limitation that can't be fixed. Just as he was born with a double-jointed wrist and a brilliant cricket brain. Murali and Warnie are just two high-profile bowlers. Here are some others that can't be ignored.

Sonny Ramadhin (West Indies, 1929–)

Sonny Ramadhin was born in Trinidad and Tobago and became interested in cricket when he attended the Canadian Mission School. At the age of 21 he was selected for the West Indies 1950 tour of England where he baffled English cricketers with his ability to spin the ball both ways. With the help of Ramadhin, the West Indies went on to win their first series victory against England. Ramadhin holds the record — 774 — for the highest number of balls bowled by one player in a Test.

Glenn Donald McGrath (Australia, 1970–)

Glenn McGrath played his first Test match against New Zealand in 1993 and became Australia's first fast bowler to play 100 tests. McGrath was not an exceptionally fast bowler, but his accuracy was legendary. In 2005 he was the fourth bowler in history to take 500 Test wickets and he retired from Test cricket in December 2006. When McGrath left the Test cricket arena, he held the record for the most runs scored as a number 11 batsman. McGrath and his wife, Jane, established the McGrath Foundation in 2002 to raise money for breast care nurses in rural and regional Australia. They both were made Members of the Order of Australia for their work at the Foundation in 2008, while Glenn's contribution to cricket was also acknowledged.

Curtly Ambrose (1963–)

Curtly Elconn Lynwall Ambrose was an extraordinary bowler in that golden era of West Indian cricket during the 1980s and 1990s. Curtly was fast, produced bounce but also found movement with the seam. As an extra weapon, he frustrated batsmen with his accuracy, forcing them to defend rather than score. With these talents Curtly took 405 Test wickets and once pummelled England with 8 for just 45 runs. And at Perth's intimidating WACA ground in 1992-3 he took 7 Australian wickets for just one run! Scary stuff, but Curtly did it all quietly — no sledging from him.

Foul and fun bowling facts

- In matches over two days, the captain can take a new ball after 80 overs if he likes. The shine on the new ball is seen as an advantage. But it hasn't always helped.
- If you see the third umpire bringing a small box onto the field then that can mean only one thing. The ball is damaged or has gone badly out of shape, and another has to be chosen. The box holds used balls, and one closest matching the condition of the ball in play is picked. There's sometimes quite a long 'discussion' about which ball should be chosen.
- What happens when your ball looks the same colour as the grass? In 2007, the International Cricket Council decided that in One Day International matches, the ball should be changed after every 35 overs. This is because ODI balls are white, and look a sludgy greeny-brown after a while. You'd

never know where it was, although this can make the game even more interesting.

- Allen Stanford, one-time, and for a very short time, cricket sponsor, wanted to introduce a black bat to highlight the white one-day ball. For the moment, players are using black tape.
- Orange and yellow balls have been tried out and rejected. The latest experiments are with pink.
- You're allowed to shine the ball by rubbing it against your trousers. Bowlers shine it on one side only. This helps it to swing when it's pitched. It makes the trousers a bit pink but it's worth it.
- New Zealand now wears a lycra kit. The pants have a smooth leg for shining one side of the ball and a slightly rougher leg to keep a side matt. And there's even a little towel tucked into the waistband for wiping the bat handle.
- Myth: spin bowlers like bowling into the wind. Not true. Wind is tiring. Wind can gust and blow around, not just from one direction. There's been a lot of hot air about bowling in the wind.
- The fastest ball ever was bowled by Pakistan's Shoaib Akhtar during the 2003 World Cup on the Newlands Ground in Cape Town, South Africa. The English batsman, Nick Knight, didn't see it. No wonder, as it broke the 100 mph barrier, blasting in at 100.2 mph — that's 161.3 kph.
- In 1981 there was just one ball left to play in the One Day International between Australia and New Zealand. New Zealand had the chance to whack it and win. But

Trevor Chappell bowled it along the ground to make it unwhackable. No one was amused. It really wasn't cricket. And neither was Bodyline...

Bodyline — the watershed

'There are two sides out there. One is trying to play the game of cricket. The other is not.'

WILLIAM MALDON 'BILL' WOODFULL (1897–1965), AUSTRALIA'S CAPTAIN DURING THE 'BODYLINE' SERIES.

Australia started it all, though not the Bodyline 'technique' itself. Basically, the Australians were too good, especially their ace batsman, Don Bradman. During the 1930 Test Match in England, Bradman had helped Bill Woodfull's team to a sound Australian victory. England didn't like it and wanted revenge.

In the 1932–33 series in Australia, the upper class amateur English captain, Douglas Jardine, hatched a plan. And during the six-week voyage on the *S.S. Orontes*, he had plenty of time to share it with his team, although no one else was in on the plan. Then, during the first Test in Sydney, his plan was revealed.

His fastest bowler, Harold Larwood, sprinted hard down the pitch, rocketed a bouncer and intimidated each batsman in turn. Jardine pulled fielders close to the batsman's leg side. The next ball was another bouncer. The batsman was now so nervous that the ball ricocheted off his bat or glove and straight into the hands of a waiting leg side fielder.

The crowd was stunned. Even more so when England actually won the Test in Sydney with this 'technique'. Surely England wouldn't repeat it in Adelaide? But they did. This time, Bert Oldfield got hit on the head and fractured his skull, although he admitted that he'd sustained it through a bad shot from a normal fast delivery. This was not at all what the crowd believed at the time, and they yelled in anger and disbelief. Even more so when a ball thumped Australia's captain just above his heart.

The Australian Board of Cricket sent a reasoned telegram to England. The 'technique' carried on. As the tour progressed, politicians and diplomats in Canberra and London joined the debate. The two nations were on the brink of an international incident, and at a time when both countries least needed it, for they were both reeling from the Great Depression and their economies were sunk. The last thing they needed was a row to drag them down further.

Tempers cooled and England won the Ashes but the Bodyline technique was never repeated. Rules were made to restrict bouncers to a limited number per over. So what was the final verdict? Was Bodyline an attempt at a skill innovation — the 'Fast Leg Theory' as some English cricketers put it? Or was it an attack of madness in the face of an otherwise unbeatable Australian team? Sixty-six years later, the jury is still out.

But there are a couple of interesting points to ponder. First, Australia's captain, Bill Woodfull, never retaliated with dangerous bowling, much to his credit. Secondly, Australia had an answer to England but chose not to give it. They could have selected Eddie Gilbert — a fast and furious genuine pace bowler with accuracy and grit. So why was Gilbert not selected? The history books offer no technical reason, but it should be noted that Eddie Gilbert was an Aboriginal.

These days, Cricket Australia is trying to tap into the skills of its indigenous people and is proud of those with Aboriginal roots who have made it to the top. Like Jason Gillespie, an Australian fast bowler who is proud to say that his grandfather belonged to the Kamilaroi people.

Cricket has always mirrored life and politics, and is no stranger to all sorts of prejudice. Just ask women.

'The ICC wants cricket to be a genuinely global sport and to achieve that goal cricket has to be a genuine global sport for girls and women, as well as boys and men.'

ICC DIRECTOR JACK CLARKE.

14 Women's CRICKET

Women's cricket is in the best of health and growing in popularity among the young. In 2008 the England women's team won the One-Day Ashes in Australia in the famous Don Bradman stadium at Bowral. England fielded a team with an average age of 22, including two 18-year-olds. But how did it all begin?

Bowling beauties

English women really got stuck into their cricket in those early days! How they skied the ball and lunged at those nicks — and all before running home to cook dinner. Perhaps women took to playing cricket before the men — we don't know. Some people believe that way back in the Middle Ages early cricketers used upturned three-legged milking stools as wickets. So perhaps milkmaids skied those balls, struggled home with the milk, and then cooked dinner. By the 14th century much firmer evidence points to women enjoying the game, for there's a neat illustration of a woman bowling smartly at a man wielding a bat behind his head. So by this time, at least, both men and women enjoyed a slog together.

The birth of the modern game

We know for sure that women played team cricket in England during the 18th century, mainly in the southern counties of Surrey and Sussex. The matches were played with skill, and were well supported by betting and prizes. Winners won an array of goodies from beer to delicate lace gloves. Their skills even drew the attention of the media.

Here's an extract from *The Reading Mercury* newspaper, 26 July 1745, on a match between Bramley village and Hambledon in the county of Surrey.

> 'The greatest cricket match that was played in this part of England was on Friday, the 26th of last month, on Gosden common ... between eleven maids of Bramley and eleven maids of Hambledon, all dressed in white. The Bramley maids had blue ribbons and the Hambledon maids red ribbons on their heads. The Bramley girls got 119 notches and the Hambledon girls 127 ... The girls bowled, batted, ran and catched as well as most men could do in that game.'

There are several reports of matches played between young maidens and married women, too. It seems they became quite a fixture, with men egging on their favourite side — and of course, betting on it, too. But the greatest development came when women's village competition matches became popular among the well-to-do. Some 'Ladies of Quality and Fashion' played a match in 1777 that was even reported in the *Morning Post*. The 'Woman of the Match' award went to a 20-year-old, Elizabeth Ann Burrell. The press, her prowess and prettiness got the attention of the eighth Duke of Hamilton, who married her the next year. Perhaps it was Elizabeth's fetching cricket frock that really won the Duke for her?

What women wore

Cricket fashion has died — murdered by practicality. These days, you might see a bit of colour on club kit, or a lot of colour for the One Day or Twenty20 game. But the comfy tracksuit-style trousers and loose-fitting shirt are designed for movement and air circulation. As we've seen, 18th century maids dressed in their cricket whites — flowing long skirts with full-sleeved bodices. Teams were colour-coded with pretty, shiny silk ribbons.

In 1890, two women's touring teams, the Reds and the Blues took to the road in great style. They wore comfortable flannel blouses and long skirts but with fetching ribbons in blue or red, striped around the collar and hem. A blue or red bow held the collar in place, and a blue or red sash swept around the waist. To die for. And, alas, to trip over and restrict movement.

So by 1926, skirts were shorter, tunics ample and simple, and absolutely no prettying was allowed. Cream was the new white, although both were allowed. Sleeveless frocks and transparent stockings were not. It might seem surprising that some national teams have only just given up skirts for trousers. Perhaps they were clinging to women's cricket of the past. A time when thousands crowded round to admire skill, entertainment and perhaps, dare we these days admit, a little fashion? But cool kit alone did not develop the game during the 19th century.

Women's cricket, crowds and crime!

The fact was, that women cricketers were good at their sport. They knew the game and how to entertain, too. So England, the 'home' of cricket, became a welcome place for women as well as men during the 19th century. In 1811, the first county match took place between Surrey and Hampshire at Ball's Pond in Middlesex. The women's ages varied wildly — from 14 to 60. The match was sponsored to the tune of 1,000 guineas, and many bets were placed.

The tentacles of women's cricket spread throughout the century and across the British Isles. By 1887 at Nun Appleton in Yorkshire, the first women's cricket club was formed. The women weren't nuns. Perhaps that's why they ditched the place name and called their venture the 'White Heather Club'. All the women were posh, were the talk of Society, and drew a good clutch of fascinated spectators.

In 1890, the Original English Lady Cricketers team took full advantage of their attractive game. Also, their colourful kit, for these women were the 'Reds' and the 'Blues'. They toured England playing exhibition matches to large crowds — as many as 15,000. Very successful until the manager ran off with the money and the ladies had to return home. They must have really missed the sixpence paid for each match. But the bug had bitten, and women began to organise on a much larger scale.

Sadly, something got lost along the way — the masses of spectators. Now, only in India do truly massive crowds attend women's cricket matches. Hopefully, many other nations will follow their lead.

The Original English Lady Cricketers team, 1890.

Women around the world

Towards the end of the 18th century, and way into the 19th, British men went to the far corners of the growing Empire. As soldiers, sailors, teachers, explorers, missionaries and merchants they took their weapons, tools, briefcases, investments, artists' palettes, cricket gear and wives to all parts of the globe. Many settled, and on warm, sunlit evenings they played on pitches and socialised in clubhouses that looked exactly like the ones back home.

But the women did not only applaud politely in the stands, or cut countless rounds of cucumber sandwiches and lemon slices. They also took to the field. In some parts of the Empire, the seeds of cricket fell on very fertile feminine soil. By 1886 in New Zealand's Nelson Province, organised cricket was played with great energy. On the Indian subcontinent, many probably already had the basic skills through their ancient bat-and-ball game, gilli-danda. Across every continent, enthusiastic women set up their own clubs. The modern era of women's cricket was about to begin.

THE MODERN INTERNATIONAL ERA

1905	Victoria Women's Cricket Association in Australia formed.
1926	England Women's Cricket Association founded.
1931	Australian Women's Cricket Association established.
1934/5	First England overseas tour made to Australia and New Zealand. First Test Match played between Australia and England. England win.
1937	Australia tour England and win.
1958	International Women's Cricket Council (IWCC) created — with Australia, England, New Zealand, South Africa, the West Indies, Denmark and the Netherlands.
1973	Women's first One-Day World Cup — a competition they held before the men!
1997	The World Cup Final between Australia and England at the daunting Eden Gardens ground in India draws 80,000 spectators.

2000 Women are finally allowed into the Long Room — the private male sanctuary at England's Lord's cricket ground. But were women bothered?

2005 IWCC fully integrated with the ICC, but with their own committee to deal with women's cricket issues.

2007 The ICC announced that only the top-10 ranked Test sides would have ODI status. These sides are Australia, England, India, Ireland, the Netherlands, New Zealand, Pakistan, South Africa, Sri Lanka and West Indies. Most national women's cricket associations are now linked with the men's, while Bangladesh, India and Pakistan's are run separately.

2009 Ashes Tests between Australia and England are every bit as competitive and compelling as the men's. 2009 saw England Women retain the Ashes. Australia is bound to fight back next time. In the same year England beat New Zealand in the One Day International World Cup in Australia and then again at Lord's ground in the first Twenty20 World competition. England's year, but...

2010 You can't keep Australian women down. They beat New Zealand in a nail-biting final of the World Twenty20 competition, winning by just three runs.

With thrilling results like these and greater investment, the women's game is becoming great to play and great to watch.

This time line doesn't highlight the heroines of the game, and there are many. England's Myrtle Maclagan scored the first Test century against New Zealand on 7 January 1935. In the same Test, and with the same team, Betty Snowball reached 189 — a record unbroken for 50 years. But perhaps one of the greatest heroines is England's Christina Willes. For she influenced the men's game more than many of the men themselves, and at a time when women inventors were placed firmly in the shadows.

The round-arm rumpus

Until the early 1800s under-arm bowling was the norm. It was slow, but bowlers could use quite a lot of cunning. Wickets were bumpy and pitted, and bowlers could target these blips quite well with the slower ball — a bit like pinpointing the target jack in bowls. They could loop the ball, too, and make the batsman take a fatal swipe. That was, until about 1807 when Christina Willes decided that it was too hard to bowl under-arm because her long skirt got in the way. So, in the barn next to her home in Tonford near Canterbury, she straightened her arm, swung it around her side, and zipped the ball towards her brother.

Christina never looked back, and neither did her brother. John Willes took this technique to his club and took the credit as well. To this day, many historians refuse to believe that Christina's skirt got in the way. Perhaps they could try bowling in one and see if they still want to credit John with the new style.

Some actually suggest that it was Tom Walker who invented this faster, straighter ball in the 1790s. It's interesting how he never got much publicity for it at the time. In any case, round-arm bowling was not officially accepted until 1828. And it was a long time before over-arm bowling developed from Christina's invention. How could anyone doubt her skill with quotes like, 'Willes, his sister and his dog could beat any XI in England.'

Jhulan Goswami (India, 1983–)

Surely every young girl cricketer wants to be like Jhulan Goswami, Captain of India? In 2007 this young all-round star was the ICC Player of the Year. Her beginnings, though, were not quite as starry. As a 13-year-old she played tennis-ball cricket with boys near her house. But her bowling was too slow for them, so they shoved her into the outfield. Jhulan was unfazed and vowed to make her bowling faster — with a proper cricket ball!

Jhulan's bowling is medium right-arm, but she packs a punch with 120 kph deliveries. Many men would give their right arm for that kind of speed. She's handy with the bat, too. In the First Test against England in 2006 she took 10 wickets for only 78 runs, and helped take India to victory. Jhulan now plays for the Air India club team, for her state, Bengal, her country, India, and for the Asia XI. Those boys Jhulan played with might beg to field for her now!

There would, of course, be more Jhulan Goswamis if the women's game had better sponsorship. If women all over the world could work less at the day job and more in the nets. Slowly, drinks' manufacturers and mobile phone magnates are seeing the potential of the women's game. In Australia, Milo's sponsorship and 'Have A Go' programme have stirred huge interest at the grass roots level. More of this, and we will see an army of Jhulans in the future.

15 Cutting, nicking, EDGING ...

'I really only had one stroke, maybe, but it went to ten different parts of the field.'
— C.B. Fry

Did shepherds first hit a ball of sheep's wool with their crook? Or did milkmaids knock a cow pat with a butter-churning paddle? Until the 16th century, either suggestion could be true when regarding the origins of the bat. As the game spread, equipment became a bit more uniform. Most players batted with a flattened stick, slightly curved at the end — a bit like a hockey stick. Gradually it was straightened and flattened out. The MCC has a collection of over 200 years' worth of bats, and you can see pictures of them on the Lord's ground's website. But the oldest bat we know of is from 1729, inscribed with the initials J.C. and it is kept at the Oval ground in Kennington, south London.

There were no rules on size, though. Just imagine trying to wield a bat as wide as the stumps! Okay, it would stop the ball, but you'd never lift it to score a six. This all got sorted in 1771, when a bat's width was limited to four and a quarter inches (10.8 cm). It remains this width today.

The new bat was certainly narrower, lighter and more

streamlined. But it was made with a single piece of willow or ash and had no 'give'. So if a batsman thwacked the ball, the vibration shot through the hands and wrists. Very painful!

But the 1800s was the age of innovation. It needed to be, for bowling had changed and, with it, the need for a brand new bat. Slow under-arm bowling was dwindling. Faster round-arm bowling took over in the 1830s, and by 1862, awesomely quick over-arm bowling was given the okay.

So thank goodness for Mr Charles Goodyear, who unwittingly helped make a bat that could cope. Famous for his tyres, he discovered in 1840 how to vulcanise latex, making it supple but not sticky. The benefits seeped into many spheres of life, including cricket. Bat makers sandwiched sheets of this latex inside a cane handle. Until then, they'd used whalebone. Then they bound the handle with twine to a whippy, willow bat blade. Finally, the handle was topped off with a comfy latex grip. The handle could now absorb the shock of hitting sixes.

The tide was turning against the bowler, who until now fired most of the shots. With their new weapons, batsmen could now use the ripping ball — which returns the ball as fast as it comes in — to their advantage with good timing. Especially if the 'sweet part' — the middle of the bat — makes contact. Bats were carved and curved to create the perfect middle for the perfectly timed stroke.

Banned bats

Since this time there have been a few experiments with bats. Not all of them have stood up to MCC standards.

The weight of a bat, though, is not in the rule book and is up for grabs. In the 18th century some bats weighed over 5 lb (2.27 kg). In the 19th, this got whittled down to 4 lb (1.82 kg). Today, some batsmen choose super-heavyweight bats to slog the ball into the stands. It doesn't always work, for, as we know, timing is the real power. Then there was Dennis Lillee's famous enamelled metal effort at Perth in 1979, though he was asked to take it off the field and return with something that looked like wood. In 2005, Ricky Ponting caused a stir with a bat coated on the back with 1.55 mm of graphite, to strengthen it. The makers claimed that it was only to stop it splitting. For the annoying thing about the cricket bat is that it frays and splits just as it reaches its peak. But, in general, the cricket bat is really a classic item, not much messed with.

And if a batsman holds his chosen weapon straight and does not hit across the line of the ball, then he has a good chance of successfully hitting a stunning array of strokes and masterstrokes: hooks, glances, cuts, sweeps, reverse sweeps. And a dangerous new stroke so ably struck by Kevin Pietersen against New Zealand in 2008 — a reverse sweep with his left hand. Pietersen is a right-handed batsman, so the bowler was completely confused! Now known as the switch hit, this stroke is a favourite to watch, even when it's not very successful.

FAST FACTS

- Early on in cricket history, batsmen got sly. They stopped their wicket tumbling by getting their foot or leg to the ball first. Not really cricket. So in 1774 a law was passed to stop this happening. It was the first Leg Before Wicket (LBW) rule. And there have been arguments over LBW decisions ever since!
- A team could bat on and on, but this often meant that a game would go on and on and the chance for a side to win could be lost. So the 'declaration' was invented and a team could stop, or declare its innings and put the other team in to bat. The first team to declare was Australia in a match against England at the Kennington Oval in 1889. The match, though, could still go on and on. It wasn't until the 1930s that it was decided a few days was quite enough.

16 Batting GREATS

Who's the best batsman of all time? Statistics say one thing, personal choice another. We all have a different opinion on style and class. There is a problem with comparing batsmen according to statistics. Conditions have changed enormously for both bowlers and batsmen over the centuries. It's hardly fair to compare the manicured pitch of today with the pitted patch of days gone by. First-class cricketers now play many more matches over a season, so they tot up more first-class runs than they used to. They may play in their home country during the summer season, then go abroad to play in another league in *their* summer. Then there are always those top-paying tournaments to squeeze in, like the new Indian Players' League that burst on the scene in 2008.

Just a few fab batsmen

The following are just a few of the most mesmerising, dashing batsmen of the last century. You might say, 'Where's top-flight Ricky Ponting, Len Hutton, Denis Compton, W. G. Grace or Sunil Gavaskar?' Where is the great Garfield Sobers, my own all-time favourite? There are so many who could be mentioned. One thing really stands out about all

Australia v. India,
MCG, Melbourne,
Australia, 01/01/1948.
Don Bradman batting,
Phadkar bowling.

of these great batsmen. Most were really all-rounders. As well as their brilliant batting, they have also taken a basketful of wickets or catches or stumpings, like the true athletes they were, or still are.

The very, very best play not for themselves but for their team. They build solid partnerships that give the lower-order batsmen courage and their bowlers a fighting chance of getting the other side out. Two fine Australian batsmen set the mould for good team playing: William Lloyd 'Billy' Murdoch and Percival Stanislaus 'Percy' McDonnell, who scored the first double century stand together in 1889 against England at the Kennington Oval in south London. In the same match, Murdoch scored 211, showing that teamwork doesn't stifle individual success.

Sir Jack Hobbs (John Berry Hobbs, England, 1882–1963)

Hobbs learned his craft as a child, using a cricket stump as a bat and a tennis post for a wicket At the age of 12 he joined his first cricket team — the Church Choir Eleven at St Matthews, Cambridge. In 1903, at the age of 21, he joined the Surrey Club. He made his Test debut for England in 1908 and went on to play 61 Test matches throughout his career. Hobbs scored more first-class runs and more first-class centuries than any other cricketer even though his career was interrupted by his service in the Royal Flying Corps during World War I and by missing most of the 1921 season due to a thigh injury and appendicitis.

Victor Trumper (Australia, 1877–1915)

Victor Trumper grew up in Surry Hills, Sydney, and practised his cricket in his backyard, surrounding suburban streets and nearby Moore Park. He played with the Carlton Club at the age of 15 and with the South Sydney Club when he was 16. Trumper was a late inclusion in the 1899 team and he became the first Australian to score 300 runs in England. In 1902 he was the first batsman to score a century before lunch in Test cricket (at Old Trafford) and he earned a reputation for being able to play on the most difficult wicket. He played his final Test in Sydney in 1912. His abilities as a batsman were recognised internationally and his untimely death at the age of 37 sent shockwaves throughout the international cricketing community.

William (Bill) Harold Ponsford (Australia, 1900–1991)

Bill Ponsford was born in Melbourne, grew up in Fitzroy and played for his local grade club before moving to the St Kilda Cricket Club in 1917. Ponsford made his first-grade debut for St Kilda at the age of 15. In 1923 he was named the captain of the Victorian side that played against Tasmania, and it was in this game that Bill broke the world record for the highest individual score at that level of cricket. He was a member of the Australian side that faced the English tactics of bowling that was later to become known as Bodyline. When his teammates remarked on the amount of bruises covering his body after his time at the wicket, Ponsford remarked that he wouldn't mind a few more if it meant he could have made 100 runs.

Sir Donald George Bradman (Australia, 1908–2001)

Known as 'The Don', 'Braddles' and 'The Boy from Bowral', Don Bradman was brought up in the southern highlands of New South Wales. But being a country boy was never a setback in a land where talent will out. This giant of the game belted the ball for his country in a spell that lasted 20 years. Like most men of his age, World War II interrupted Bradman's career. Nevertheless, he played in 52 Test matches and scored an average 99.94 runs. The Don moved like a train towards the ball and was brazen in the face of fast bowlers. At England's Headingley ground he made a stunning 309 in just one day. His greatest fear was a spin bowler on a 'sticky dog' pitch — hot sun after a heavy rain. England's Hedley Verity, with his leg-breaks and googlies, was Don's idea of a nightmare. Bradman has received just about every honour that Australia could give him, and is the only Australian to have a museum dedicated to his achievements while he was still alive.

Walter Reginald Hammond (England, 1903–1965)

Wally Hammond was born in the coastal town of Dover, in the ancient cricketing county of Kent. At 20 he played for Gloucestershire and became well-known as a strong driver of the ball. His straight bat was classic. But he could hook, glance, cut and loft with the best of them. He played in 85 Tests, scored 22 centuries, 24 half centuries with a total average of 58.45 runs. As a medium-fast bowler he took 83 wickets. A great fielder, he caught or stumped 110 hapless international batsmen.

Brian Charles Lara (West Indies, 1969–)

Simply known as 'The Prince', Brian Lara has broken just about every record in the book, then broken it again when it was lost to some pretender to his throne. His stance is daring. He holds himself forward over a bent knee, his eyes level and peering straight ahead, the bat raised high behind him, just waiting to smash the ball to the boundary. With this attacking technique, Brian Lara has secured an average of 52.88 runs in 131 Test matches. He has the most runs in an over — 28. The highest score in a Test match innings — 400. A world record 501 runs for a first-class team — England's Warwickshire County. As a captain, he tried to stir a West Indies team that had waned towards the end of the last century. His commitment was unequalled. He even starred in the field, taking 164 Test catches. Brian Lara has retired from the international game, has since been a great Ambassador for Sport for his nation, Trinidad and Tobago, and still plays cricket.

Sachin Tendulkar (India, 1973–)

'Tendlya', 'Little Master', 'Maestro' — these are just some of the loving nicknames for this small but astounding batsman. 'Liquid Gold' would be a good choice, for he floats and glides the ball around the ground as smoothly as a river flows into the sea. He balances perfectly, he anticipates, then strokes and guides the ball around the ground. Sachin Tendulkar scored his first Test century at the tender age of 17. It was a brave innings. But then, he had already shown his strength of character. At just 16, a blaster ball from Pakistan's class fast bowler, Waqar Younis, bloodied his nose. But the young Tendulkar just carried on.

Stephen Rodger Waugh (Australia, 1965–)

Known as 'Tugga' or the 'Ice Man', Steve Waugh was a natural, free-flowing batsman; a joy to watch. Once dubbed 'the ultimate evolved cricketer', he played in 168 Test matches for his country, more than any other cricketer. His average was 51.06 — a staggering figure for a batsman placed in the middle order, a place from where he could command a match. But he was even greater in the One Day Internationals, where his style shone. He also took 92 wickets as a medium pace bowler, and 112 catches or stumpings. At his last Test match in Sydney, the promoters gave the crowd hundreds of red-and-white spotted handkerchiefs. Just like the ones Waugh wiped his bat with.

Jacques Henry Kallis (South Africa, 1975–)

South Africa's Jacques Kallis is a formidable right-hand batsman. He combines well-timed flourish with a set of keen defensive strokes. This is a man who wants to stay in and build his innings. For this some have accused him of being another 'grazer', like England's Geoffrey Boycott (1940-). But he is the only player ever to get over 10,000 runs plus 200 wickets and 100 catches in both Test and One Day Internationals. The blogs buzzed when he was made Wisden's International Cricketer of the Year in 2007. 'Kallis? Such a selfish batsman!' and, 'Is the number of partners he's run out one of the statistics?' also, 'Okay, he's got great averages, but is he much of a match winner?' But then, 'He holds the fastest Test 50 in history, from 24 balls.' He's also scored 31 Test centuries — that's one more than Don Bradman.

Martin Crowe (New Zealand, 1962–)

Martin and his brother Jeff both represented New Zealand at international level, while Martin was Wisden's Cricketer of the Year in 1985. His career as a right-hand batsman with New Zealand spanned 16 years. During his time as captain in the 1992 World Cup, New Zealand only lost two matches. Throughout his career, Martin Crowe scored nearly 20,000 runs, including a total of 71 centuries. Since his retirement as a player, Crowe has gone on to work as a commentator and has become a board member of the South Sydney Rabbitohs Rugby League Football Club, which is part-owned by his cousin, Russell Crowe.

Umesh Valjee (England, 1970–)

Umesh Valjee is a talented batsman who has played 54 matches for England Deaf Cricket since 1992, 41 of them as captain. He has scored 2639 Test runs with an average of 49 and has a 47 average in One Day Internationals. In 2011 Umesh blasted three centuries against Australia to secure the Deaf Ashes and Twenty20 series. In the same year he received the England Disability Cricket Award. But Valjee has also achieved outside Deaf Cricket — making it as a 2nd XI player for top counties Hampshire and Gloucestershire, and touring for the MCC.

Innovations and stunning innings

But it's all such an individual choice. Perhaps it's as fair to remember the innovators, like Australia's Michael Slater. Here was a man who didn't bother easing himself into a Test innings — he just belted the ball from the start and created a tempo for the whole team. Or perhaps a single innings shoots a batsman up there with the 'greats', like Adam Gilchrist's mesmerising century for Australia during the second Test at Perth during the 2006/07 Ashes. He was, of course, his own brilliant self. But wasn't there a glimpse of Viv Richards lofting the ball straight and into the stands? And Gary Sobers' graceful square cut? The ease of the 'Champagne Batsman', David Gower, languidly hooking it for four? Gilchrist's Test century was second in speed only to the great Viv Richards, who gets the last word on the subject.

The last word

Let's give it up for the West Indies' Sir Isaac Vivian Alexander Richards, otherwise known as 'Master Blaster', 'Smokey', or just plain Viv (1952–). After all, he did score 8540 Test runs in 121 Tests with a staggering average of 50.23 runs. He also featured large in the first World Cup of 1975, where he helped the West Indies to a win. And again in 1979. A mean fielder and cunning off-spin bowler, it is no surprise that he was one of Wisden's Cricketers of the Century in the year 2000. What's more, he did it in such a powerfully relaxed way — and always chewing gum. He needed to be strong. For right at the outset, bowlers were out to sledge him...

Greg Thomas (1960–) of England pounded a bouncer at a young, slightly anxious Viv Richards. Viv stepped forward, swung at the ball and missed.

'It's red, it's round. Can't you see it?' taunted Thomas.

The next ball stuck three-quarters down the pitch and whizzed off past the leg stump.

'It's red, it's round and it weighs four-and-a-half ounces,' Thomas quipped.

Viv Richards loosened his arms and faced the next ball. Thomas whacked it straight into the slot. Viv struck the ball sweetly in the middle of the bat and lofted it over the boundary, the ground, and into the river. He turned to Greg Thomas, smiled slowly and said, 'You know what it looks like. Now go get it!'

Sledging

Sledging is when batsmen and bowlers needle each other on the pitch. They try to chip away at each other's confidence and make fun of their opponent's mistakes. It can be light-hearted, but there's a growing unease that it has become a bit too personal and is damaging the game. Many of the exchanges are unrepeatable, but a few are just clever.

The West Indies pace bowler, Malcolm Marshall had just taken two of India's top batsmen for no runs. India's best batsman, Sunil Gavaskar, had put himself in at number four, instead of his usual opening position, in an effort to pull the side together. Gavaskar walked to the crease, his team in tatters and Marshall just shook his head saying, 'Man, it don't matter where you come in to bat, the score's still going to be zero.'

‘I don't want to do the batsman permanent injury, just cause him concern...’
So said Dennis Lillee, pictured right bowling.

17 Silly POINT

There are slips, where the ball can so easily slip out of your hand. There's the gully, where you really want the ground to swallow you up if you drop that vital catch. Then there's deep mid-wicket — a long way from the thick of the fray in the outfield. All these are field placings, which evolved centuries ago from a game played on a bumpy field with real gullies to negotiate.

Cat-and-mouse

Placing fielders is an art, a science, which takes experience and gut instinct. A good captain controls the batsman as much as he can by positioning his fielders to tame and intimidate, or to lure the batsman into making a mistake. At the same time, he has to consider which placings will match each bowler's talents and tactics.

The craft of the batsman is to elude the field and pin it to the back fence. The response of the fielder then is to close in, leap and chase. Or hang slyly around the boundary for a scooped ball and a dolly catch. It's a cat-and-mouse part of the game, and deadly serious — nearly literally sometimes, when the slip fielders stand very close to the bat as they often do in a tense one-day game.

Short but powerful

The 50-over One Day International has changed the face of field placing and tactics as it has many other features of the game. When the first 'power play' rule was introduced, only two fielders were allowed outside the 30-yard circle that surrounded the pitch. This brought about some very exciting play, as batsmen could start the game by blasting the ball over the close fielders and getting some quick runs. After that, they had to be more careful where they put the ball.

But in 2005, new power play rules allowed one power play session for the first 10 overs. The captain could choose two more 5-over sessions depending on how the game was going or who was batting. The timing of power play has been crucial in intensifying pressure on the batsmen at the right time. Cat-and-mouse again! But whatever the tactics, there's always someone who never quite knows when the captain will call him on. And that's the Twelfth Man.

The Twelfth Man

It sounds like a thriller, and sometimes it is. A team's Twelfth Man is a bit of a spare part. He comes and goes on the pitch as other fielders go off for a bit. Sometimes it's for something serious, like a concussed slip fielder. But mostly it's just for a finger plaster or a desperate run to the Gents. Usually, the Twelfth Man is stuck on the boundary until the player returns. But just occasionally, he becomes a hero and makes the match-winning catch way out on the boundary.

Sometimes teams have been accused of using their Twelfth Man as a tactic, which isn't at all cricket. At others, the Twelfth Man has been caught dreaming as the Eleventh Man trots back on the field. Like in 1986 when India's Laman Ramba stayed on the pitch for a whole over until someone noticed that his team had one man more than they should! By the way, if you Google 'Twelfth Man' you're likely to get a lot of hits for the Australian sports' spoof, Billy Birmingham, who just loves to lampoon the game and its commentators.

Looking silly

It's required. All fielders understand that their missed catches and slip-ups on greasy outfields are part of the agony and the entertainment. Sometimes that fumbled catch or ill-timed frontal splat on the outfield has lost matches, series and honour. But generally, it's just a blip. The job of many long positions seems to be to catch stray dogs, pigeons and even large brown inflatable sausages.

The safest pairs of hands

Slip fielding is dangerous, especially first slip, which is frighteningly close to the batsman. It's a really specialist position and needs practice and fitness. Here are some sizzling slip catchers.

WORLD'S TOP FIVE INTERNATIONAL SLIP CATCHERS

Top man	Top tally
Mark Waugh (Australia)	181
Mark Taylor (Australia)	157
Allan Border (Australia)	156
Greg Chappell (Australia)	122
Viv Richards (West Indies)	122

Behind the wicket

It can only go wrong. Crouched behind the wicket, keepers have always been hidden from sight until the last second. Misses always seem to stay in the mind far longer than breathtaking catches. For a long time, it just wasn't seen as a job. That was until keepers like the great George Pinder 'Hattersley'.

Stopping the long-stop

For generations, any old plodder got dumped behind the wicket. There seemed no point putting anyone good there just to stick an arm out occasionally. Most teams employed a 'long-stop' position, way behind the wicket-keeper, to mop up all the wicket-keeper's misses. That was, until George Pinder Hattersley (1841–1903) of Yorkshire.

As a boy, young George was a hard-working pocketknife grinder. As a man, he was a razor-sharp, athletic wicket-keeper, who always 'stood up' to the ball fearlessly. George stopped most loose balls and stumped batsmen ruthlessly. He was so good that the long-stop fielding position was becoming a waste of a fielder. Nevertheless, George felt safe with someone backing him up.

But in a match between the North and South of England, captain A.N. Hornby told George to do without one. George was nervous. He felt a deep, icy chill between his back and the long boundary. He coped, but rather miserably. So the long-stop was reinstated.

Finally, during a match at The Oval, George realised that perhaps he was good enough to stand alone. That the long-stop was a thing of the past. His teammate, Ephraim Lockwood, got dazedly bored doing nothing way out there on the far boundary. So in the end he shook his head and stomped off to a different position, calling out,

'Nay, George!' called Ephraim, 'I've been behind thee for twenty-three overs and had nowt to stop. I'm off where there's summat to do!' And so the noble position of wicket keeping was born.

The secret of George's success? Natural ability, hard work and Tom Emmet. Tom was George's teammate up at Yorkshire County. He pitched power-packed balls that zipped towards the leg stump but then whizzed off toward the off stump. The batsman was totally bamboozled, and George was terrified. Because these balls were great when they hit the wicket. But Tom sent a lot of them very wide, giving George plenty of diving practice. The development of fast bowling and the skill and dynamism of George Hattersley helped promote wicket-keeping to the status it holds today.

And Tom? He gave these lightning leg-breaks a name: the 'sostenuter'.

Fab five wicket-keepers

Who are the greatest wicket-keepers of all time? Everyone has his or her favourites. It's hard to compare statistics as today's cricketers play far more internationals matches. But here are a few keepers who leap like lemurs and hold their catches.

Mark Verdon Boucher (South Africa, 1976–) Probably the best current keeper, he has taken 453 Test catches and 22 stumpings.

Thomas Godfrey Evans (England, 1920–1999) Remembered for his lightning reactions and impossible leaps. He took 173 Test catches and 46 stumpings.

Adam Craig Gilchrist (Australia, 1971–) Also known as 'Gilly' or 'Church'. He retired in 2008 but took 379 Test catches and 37 stumpings, and had an amazing 17 Test centuries with the bat and one 200.

Ian Andrew Healy (Australia, 1964–) He took 366 Test catches and 29 stumpings.

Alan Philip Eric Knott (England, 1946–) Also known as 'Knotty' or the 'Flea'. He took 250 Test catches, 19 stumpings and was a very useful bat. His captain, Colin Cowdrey said of him, 'I think he is the most gifted and dedicated cricketer one could ever play with, never satisfied with his performance and always seeking for a little more perfection.' Top tip — he warmed his hands with hot water before play.

Catches to remember

It's hard to describe all those gobsmacking catches, when a fielder dives backwards, or parallel with the ground. A double catch is quite sensational to watch. A blistering ball bounces out of the fielder's hands and then he manages to catch it again. But we can do even better than that. During the tension of a 2003 One-Day World Cup, Australia's Brad Hogg launched a full toss at Pakistan's Younis Khan. Khan walloped it frantically and sent the ball straight into the hands of Ricky Ponting. Damien Martyn caught the bat! For all of these amazing feats, fielders have to be extremely fit.

All-round good players

We've looked at some of the best batsmen, bowlers and wicket-keepers, but what of the legendary all-rounders of the game. Here are just a few.

Lord Learie Nicholas Constantine (Trinidad and Tobago, 1901–1971)

Lord Learie Constantine was born in Trinidad and became famous as an 'all-round' cricketer: a powerful batsman, a devastating bowler and keen-eyed fieldsman. He captained the West Indies team against England in 1943 and brought an action against the Imperial Hotel in Russell Square when he and his family were refused admittance due to the colour of their skin. Constantine was awarded £5 in damages, but, more importantly, the case became a turning point in the struggle against racism in Britain. He was the first High Commissioner from Trinidad and Tobago to the UK.

Denis Charles Scott Compton (England, 1918–1997)

Denis Compton scored his first Test century at the age of 19 against an Australian team captained by Don Bradman. Compton's emergence as a player coincided with a time when England was desperate for some success on the international cricket scene. He gained notoriety for his risk-taking as a batsman and was an effective bowler, taking 622 wickets over his career. The rivalry between Compton and Australian player, Keith Miller, was recognised in 2005 with the creation of the Compton-Miller medal to be awarded to the Player of the Series in an Ashes clash. After retiring from cricket, Compton went on to have an occasional career as a commentator for the BBC, and wrote pieces for the Sunday Express.

Sir Frank Mortimer Maglinne Worrell (West Indies, 1924–1967)

Frank Worrell played for the West Indies and made his debut in 1947 against the English team. In 1960 he became the first black captain to skipper the entire Test series. Worrell played 51 Tests and clocked up 9 Test centuries. Worrell is reported to have been a superstitious man. When he was bowled out first ball during the 1951 tour of England, he made a fresh start in the second innings by dressing in a completely new uniform, hoping to change his luck. (Unfortunately, out first ball again!) The Frank Worrell trophy was created as a perpetual trophy to be presented to the winning captain of each Test series between Australia and the West Indies and is considered to be one of the most prestigious trophies today. Worrell was knighted for his services to cricket in 1964.

Keith Ross Miller (Australia, 1919–2004)

Keith Miller may have been one of Australia's greatest players in Test cricket, but as a child he dreamed of becoming a jockey. Miller was small for his age but a growth spurt during his teen years saw him reach the height of 6′ 2″ (188 cm), which meant giving up this dream. Instead, he turned to cricket and was selected for Melbourne High School's first XI at the age of 14. He went on to make his test debut in Australia's first Test match against New Zealand in 1946. Miller had the best statistics for an all-rounder at the time of his retirement from Test Cricket in 1956 and is one of only three Australian cricketers to have a portrait in the Lord's Long Room. Not content to rest on his laurels as a cricketer, Miller also played 50 footy matches in the VFL for St Kilda and represented Victoria in 1946.

Fighting fit

> *'In my day, 58 beers between London and Sydney would have virtually classified us as teetotallers.'*
> IAN CHAPPELL.

Is cricket the only sport you can play and still gain weight? Are cricketers only interested in the 'good life'? Ugly rumours — not totally true. More likely, cricket encourages people of all shapes and sizes to take part. Actually among the skills required by cricket are great flexibility of the fingers and hands, brilliant hand-eye coordination and timing. Perfect powers of concentration. Yes, and fitness.

But not necessarily a sprinter's shape. Not unless you're a genuine pace bowler.

There are many injuries sustained through cricket. You need to twist, crouch and spring, which messes with your knees, hips and groin. Then there are the stress fractures of the pace bowler, with his relentless pounding and arm swinging. So with all this agony, not to mention sunburn and thirst, these are some ways cricketers keep going.

FITNESS FOR THE FEARLESS OR FOOLHARDY

- **Stretching, star jumps and sprinting.**
  Weights in winter and warm-ups for net practice. Traditional, but jolly good.
- **Football, rugby, tennis, general kick about.**
  Fun and energetic, but do they build the right muscles? And the right mentality?
- **Bikram yoga.**
  Yoga exercises conducted in a minimum of 38 degrees Centigrade. For the serious cricketer. Strengthens both body and mind. Prepares cricketers from chilly climes for tropical conditions.
- **Ayurvedic herbal massage treatment.**
  Good for those tired muscles. Calms and prepares the mind.
- **Colour therapy.**
  To encourage normal and healthy workings of the body.

- **Trion-2 'magic' band, made of super-strength magnets.** Supposed to increase blood flow around the body, improving concentration levels and body cell regeneration. James Anderson of England, fresh from his ball-swinging six-wicket haul against New Zealand, has been a great fan of the band. He reckons that it helps him cope with long training sessions.
- **Letter-writing.** Exercises the fingers? Australia's Mike Hussey concentrates a lot on the mental side of the game. He writes letters to himself about particular problems concerning his technique or form. No need to block his mailbox with sympathetic postcards, though. He does have friends.

Packer kept them fit

Fitness training shot into the modern era as a result of Kerry Packer's World Cricket Series. His matches were all one day, and there were an awful lot of them played back-to-back. Innings were fast, furious, and employed some of the greatest fast bowlers ever, including the likes of Dennis Lillee and Joel Garner. Pace bowling was entertaining. So were slogged sixes and athletes chasing fours to the boundary. And wicket-keepers leaping and diving to stop 90-mile-an-hour wide balls. In short, everyone had to be fit.

Safety came on in leaps and bounds, too. The nature of the game changed. It would now and forever feature a fast game with plenty of pace and bounce. Helmets were worn and became part of the colourful uniform that showed off Packer's men. Before this time, only the brilliant English batsman, Elias Henry 'Patsy' Hendren (1889–1962) experimented with helmets — and he made them himself! Packer's men inspired the modern design, especially Graham Yallop, who was the first to sport one on 11 March 1978, against the West Indies in Bridgetown, Barbados. Well, he *was* facing some of the most punishing pace bowling of all time.

18 Cricket's control FREAKS

All sports need umpires, especially cricket, which has to deal with some very large cricketing characters as well as a long, complicated game. By at least the 17th century, umpires were part of the furniture. So, too, were scorers, who sat high on their grassy mounds counting runs and notching them up on a piece of wood. By the 18th century, the scorecard was invented, like the one now displayed at the Vine Club in Sevenoaks, Kent. But notching continued well into the 19th century. There's more to controlling a cricket game than counting runs, though.

A hard job, but someone's got to do it

Umpires have a tough life. There are 42 rules in cricket and it must be hard to remember them all, especially as there are a lot of sneaky little extras in them, or clauses. Even seasoned players sometimes struggle to tell you all 10, or is it really 11, ways of being called 'Out!'

Then there's the ICC's Code of Conduct, with 26 ways of getting fined, banned or both. But if you don't gamble on your own match, appeal too loudly and too often, throw a ball or other missile at another player, then you'll probably be okay. And if not, someone will tell you. That 'Someone' is, of course, the umpire. You can be sure that he will remind you of all the rules, codes and etiquettes that this game has gathered over the centuries.

QUICK CRICKET UMPIRING UPDATE

- In this century, the modern international game requires two field umpires, a third umpire who sits in a box watching video replays, and a fourth umpire.
- The fourth umpire really has pulled the short straw. He brings the drinks onto the field for the two utterly exhausted field umpires. A tough job, but someone's got to do it.
- The fourth umpire also has to organise the other umpires, requirements, including their trip: transport, hotels, entertainment... the list goes on.
- A referee sits in judgement on the cricketers' general behaviour. If necessary, he enforces the ICC's Code of Conduct.
- In 2000, the ICC celebrated the millennium with a brand new 'Spirit of Cricket', which is just another way of telling cricketers how to behave.

Umpires' antics

'You put your right leg in, your right leg out,
in-out, in-out, and shake it all about.'

So goes the song. Surely it must have been written for cricket umpires? If you don't know the game you might wonder what umpires are waving their arms and legs for. You might think they're just doing some much-needed exercise because they don't do much running around. One umpire stands by the bowler, and the other at square leg near the batsmen and the only exercise they get is when they change ends after each over. This is why and how they flex their muscles to stop them cramping up:

- A 'dead' ball is one that isn't in play, and is held for safekeeping in the wicket-keeper's hands. How did it die? The umpire judges several causes. Mostly, it's a ball that slips out of the bowler's hand and dribbles along the grass. Sometimes it gets stuck in the batsman's pads, or other more personal items of clothing. Whatever the reason, the umpire signals a dead ball by drooping his arms down towards his knees and swaying them across each other.

- A 'no-ball' is called when a bowler's front foot steps beyond the popping crease as he releases the ball. Or the back foot strays outside the return, or side crease. Maybe the bowler whams a 'beamer', which is a dangerous ball. Perhaps the wicket keeper or a close fielder has brushed against the batsman or his bat? For all these sins and many more, the umpire thrusts his arm out horizontally.

- 'Out!' is simply a raised arm and pointed finger. No mistake and absolutely no arguing! The more sadistic umpires will make the batsman wait a while before they raise their finger.

- On a more positive note, for hitting a six, the umpire hoists both arms above his head.
- A four gets a wave of the arm that starts with the hand bent towards the chest then swung out to the side — a bit like a door opening. Some umpires flutter their fingers as they go, or move their hand in a series of rippling waves.

Some umpires have made their movements into an art form.

Billy's ballet

Take New Zealand's Brent Fraser Bowden, aka 'Billy' Bowden (1963–). Retired from cricket due to arthritis, which struck when he was just 21, 'Billy' took to the field as an umpire. He signals 'Out!' with a crooked arthritic finger, sticks a leg out when he signals a four or a six, and a 'wide' is a ballet arabesque. Bowden himself says his signals are 50 per cent due to his arthritis and 50 per cent to entertainment value. Some cricketers are less than impressed. In 2005 Australian players voted him the worst umpire of the year. Yet he has since been given a place on the Emirates Panel of International Umpires. And he was made fourth umpire in the final of the 2007 World Cup. Whatever the criticisms, Billy possibly didn't deserve to be knocked flat out by a ball socked from Geraint Jones' bat in the 2006 Ashes.

Chancers and chuckers

There is an old saying that 'rules are made to be broken', although that is not true for cricket. But that doesn't stop some players feeling the urge to 'push the rules' a little. Like seam picking and ball gouging. Like roughing up a ball with a bit of dust in the pocket, which someone once said was 'just to dry the fingers'. Like a bowler ploughing into a batsman as he takes a run.

'Chucking' is all about elbow flexion. Basically, a true ball is delivered with a straight arm if possible. If it isn't *exactly* straight as the bowler swings his arm around, then that's okay. Just so long as he doesn't try to straighten it and therefore give the ball an extra thrust. In other words, there should be no elbow flexion. Otherwise the umpire says it's been 'thrown' or 'chucked', not bowled. There's a problem with this, though. With new technology, we now know that most bowlers deliver with at least a little flexion. So today it is generally accepted that a plus 15 per cent flexion tolerance is okay. But it's really up to the umpire on the day. Would we really want constant referrals to video analysis of multiple camera angles, and computer simulations? But at least new technology helps put to rest the arguments surrounding the arm action of some of cricket's best bowlers.

Umpires in the hot seat

In 2008 Australian umpire, Darrell Hair, strolled back onto the pitch after being suspended from duty by the ICC. So what led to this suspension?

In September 2006, a match between England and

Pakistan was well under way. The ball was getting a bit old and looked like a dog had got hold of it. So Darrell Hair picked it up and rolled it around in his hand. Then he summoned Pakistan's Inzamam ul-Haq and accused him of ball tampering, which means damaging the ball so that the batsman finds it harder to play. Inzamam walked off the pitch with the rest of the Pakistan team in tow. The air was tense. England was awarded five extra runs for having to hang around. Pakistan were outraged and refused to continue. England won the Test with no further play required.

A flurry of accusations followed: that there was racism in umpiring; that some national sides were *always* being accused; that some bowlers ball-tampered persistently. The ICC took charge and started an investigation. Then, like a bolt out of the blue, Hair offered to retire as long as the ICC paid him $500,000. They refused.

In the meetings that followed, the ICC decided that Inzamam was innocent. Darrell Hair was banned from the Elite Umpires Panel. And for refusing to return to the pitch, Inzamam suffered a four-match ban — the smallest punishment for the offence. The ICC, often scorned, had taken charge and acted boldly. The ultimate umpire had shaken its fist. But just a couple of seasons later, Hair was reinstated to the ICC's elite Emirates Panel of Umpires. The ICC itself continues to be questioned on its judgment and sense of justice.

It just isn't fair play

When the umpires put away their notepads, pull up

stumps and call 'Rain stop play!' the match is a draw. How depressing is that? Especially in a One-Day game when your team is so *obviously* going to win? It could be worse. Your team could go back on the pitch after a rain shower and have a great chance of winning, but officials have other ideas. This is exactly what happened to South Africa's One Day International team. It was 1992 and the World Cup was in full swing. South Africa had reached the semi-final and the match was in its last breathtaking moments. They needed 22 runs in just 13 overs to beat England's total. It was possible. But then, rain stopped play.

When the players took to the pitch again, the match had to be shortened, obviously. But officials calculated that the South Africans now needed 21 runs from JUST ONE BALL! Which was an impossible task. South Africa lost, and England went on, only to lose to Pakistan in the final, by 22 runs.

One good thing came out of this match. The rules for recalculating targets after a stoppage just had to change. Messers Duckworth and Lewis took up the challenge.

Duckworth–Lewis and a lot of serious maths

There was always a team that lost out when rain stopped play. Comparing the rate at which both teams scored runs just didn't work. Neither had other systems based on runs alone. None of them took account of the number of wickets that had fallen. But help was at hand. Two statistics whiz-kids — Frank Duckworth and Tony Lewis — decided to build on a project by a student from the University of West England. From this, they developed a calculation based on the number of overs left to play and the number of wickets lost. It's actually a lot more brain busting than this! But at the end of it, the Duckworth–Lewis table enabled officials to look up what the batting team would need to score. And it was certainly more possible than 21 runs from just one ball.

Nothing is perfect. Some critics say the system's way too complicated. Others that wickets lost are given too much importance. So if a team sees dark clouds looming, they'll play safe just to keep enough wickets in hand. But many spectators find it thrilling, for they get a spine-tingling end to the match.

Since the early days, the Duckworth–Lewis method has been refined. The 2004 revisions included two versions — a Standard one for your local cricket match, and a Professional one for all those number crunchers on the international scene.

Umpiring under pressure

Umpiring has changed radically since the 1990s with the use of television technology and the third umpire. There can be rather a lot of disputes in cricket, especially over a ball hitting a bat, or pad, or was it the batsman's elbow? Umpires on the ground can refer 'upstairs' to the third umpire to check out infra-red Hot Spot technology that pinpoints exactly where the ball made contact. The Snickometer — or 'Snicko' — loved by television pundits, can pick out a nick that the naked ear just cannot hear. But what made that nick? It is just not clear enough for the third umpire to use.

Hawk Eye, though, is now relied on to help judge that tricky Leg Before Wicket decision. Again, this is television technology at its best. A computer tool that tracks the continuing trajectory of a ball. Would the ball have hit the stumps if the batsman had not stuck his leg in the way? Hawk Eye knows. Or does it? Can it judge whether a ball will swerve slightly or dip a little with the wind or the moisture in the air? Not yet. But Hawk Eye is now an established part of umpiring.

Hawk Eye, Hot Spot and the mysterious third umpire can now be called upon under the Umpire Decision Review System (UDRS). Both fielding teams and batsmen can query and refer a limited number of decisions to the third umpire and his state-of-the art equipment. A Test match between New Zealand and Pakistan in 2009 saw the first use of UDRS in the top-flight arena. It was not until January 2011 that the system was rolled out to One Day Internationals, starting with a clash between England and Australia.

Not every country has signed up fully to UDRS in the domestic game. India is still holding back — but for how long? Some cricketers and cricket lovers believe that it is best to let umpires on the ground do their jobs and for players to accept their decisions — especially in heated moments, when the pitch is charged with the emotions of 13 passionate players.

'One-day cricket is an exhibition.
Test cricket is an examination.'
— Henry Blofeld

19 Short FOCUS

It's 5 January 1971, the middle of Australia's cricket season, in Melbourne, where the weather often delivers 'four seasons in one day'. But on this day there was only rain. The third test match between Australia and England at the MCG was abandoned and the spectators clearly showed their disappointment. So the two sides decided to please the crowd with a one-day game. And please them they did. In fact, the 46,000 paying spectators were delighted. And the rest is history — the history of the one-day international game.

A day to remember

One-day, or limited-over, games had been around for a while. England's first-class county teams had been playing these 40 to 60-over tournaments since 1962. They were fast, so selection was different from a Test team. Sloggers got a chance to shine. Outstanding fielders suddenly became heroes as much as bowlers and batsmen. Different rules began to develop, too. For instance, each of five bowlers only able to bowl ten overs in a 50-over game. They affected the number of overs each bowler could deliver, for example. This of course affects tactics. Do you blast the first few overs with a seamer? Or do you save their overs for the end, when there is a lot of fast scoring? Could they get the last few wickets with some sizzlers? Or would a canny spinner stop them hitting the ball for six?

So by the time international teams took an interest in the format, there was already a blueprint. It did not take long for the ODI to become a well-loved cricket institution. The first ODI World Cup took place in England in 1975 and was won by the West Indies. Everyone had such a great time that it has been repeated every four years since. A slightly lower profile World Championship slots in between.

But the beauty of the one-day game is its flexibility. Countries, first class teams and clubs alike can hold a tournament for two or three sides without a lot of fuss. The ICC has also given Test teams, first class teams, and smaller cricketing nations the chance to play each other. Their statistics all count towards personal and team records. They also count towards the smaller nations' ratings. Through the one-day game they have the chance to be noticed. To climb the ladder from being, say, an Affiliate ICC member to an Associate member.

The one-day game is an adaptable format, too. In the latest 20-over version — the Twenty20 test teams field five bowlers, who each deliver four overs. Pro-Cricket in America uses just four bowlers with five overs each. Again, it allows nations with fewer resources and players to take part. All these nations are improving fast, and the one-day game has a lot to do with it. Test nations had better watch out!

Short statistics

World Cup Cricket is the ODI with bells on. Players are as tense as wires on a suspension bridge. It certainly shows at times, too. Like in 2003, when New Zealand's Andre Adams (1975–) bowled a double bouncer. It's actually quite a hard thing to achieve when you're trying! But his tight arm just couldn't help it. And Australia's Andy Bishel punished it with a six. There are some sizzling statistics in the one-day game, but not all of them are made during World Cups...

- The best first class bowling figures belong to Rahul Sanghvi of Delhi. He took 8 wickets for 15 runs against Himachal Pradesh.
- The most runs in an over belong to Herschelle Gibbs of South Africa in the West Indies 2007 World Cup. He hit six sixes off Dan van Bunge of the Netherlands.
- The highest team score is United's 630 runs for 5 wickets against Bay Area in California in 2006.

The one-day game owes a lot to that daring and dynamic cricket lover — Kerry Packer.

'Cricket the world over, I don't think, will ever know how different things would be without Kerry Packer.'

Tony Greig

20 Packing a PUNCH

And it's Australia again! One man changed the whole image of cricket for all time, and he wasn't a famous cricketer, but he was an Australian. For Kerry Packer, the point of sport was to entertain — to make people love it; and to make money from it. And that's exactly what he achieved with cricket, especially the one-day game.

Kerry Packer was a media mogul. He owned many businesses including a cattle ranch the size of Belgium and, crucially, a television company. In 1977 the Australian Cricket Board (now Cricket Australia) refused to sell him the rights to screen Australian Test matches, even though he was offering a healthy $1.5 million Australian dollars to do so. But Kerry Packer was not easily beaten by what he thought was snobbery and some very bad economics. Why shouldn't cricket be more commercial and attract a different audience?

So Packer created his own league — the World Cricket Series — which he could televise himself. In the midst of mayhem and journalists behaving like wounded crocodiles, 50 brave cricketers signed up for the Packer party. Some of the matches were five-day tests. But Packer soon realised that the most attractive and lucrative were the one-day limited-over games, played at night in front of a packed house, with floodlights, white balls and black sightscreens. Cricketers wore bright 'clown suits' or 'pyjamas', as sniffy traditionalists called the new cricket gear. And there was the rare spectacle of helmets. With top pay and a chance to reach a wider audience, Packer's 'bandits' cared little about the sneering criticisms.

At first, the matches looked a bit scrappy and the spectators seemed unconvinced. Then, on 16 December, 1977, the great West Indian bowler, Andy Roberts, blasted a bouncer at Australian David Hookes and cracked his jaw. There's nothing like a broken bone or two for stirring the spectators and luring more to the gate.

Crowds like the 50,000 in Sydney soon loved it. The cranky journalists and stuffy cricket establishment learned to live with it. Packer's cricket circuses thrilled their audience for two years, with rogue test matches but especially, the one-day wonders. Then, in 1979, the Australian Cricket Board gave in to Packer's Channel Nine, and sold rights to televise cricket for ten years. Limited-over cricket all over the world changed for all time. It became jazzier and possibly a bit brash. But it thrilled with its tension and bite.

Mixed feelings

But Packer left a bitter taste for some. He had lured international cricketers away from their national teams, leaving many teams threadbare. England captain, Tony Greig, was one of the first and most notorious to join

Packer's pack and his country's press found it hard to forgive. There were many others as well, including greats like Dennis Lillee, Joel Garner and Imran Khan.

Packer broke a sporting boycott and sent a team to South Africa, too, and at a most sensitive time. South Africa's white minority regime had just brutally put down a demonstration in the African township of Soweto. A local leader, Steve Biko, had been cruelly murdered by the state.

But Packer expanded cricket's supporter-base by repackaging the game in a more exciting, entertaining form. And all came good in the end. Kerry Packer rewarded players like Tony Greig, who is now a cricket commentator with Packer's Nine Network. And the national teams who had lost their stars? Well, they were forced to advance their younger players. To dig deep and finally make cricket development at the grass roots a priority, which was not such a bad thing. And many of the pack returned to their national teams sharper, fitter and wiser. As Richie Benaud, a great Australian player and commentator said, 'It's because of what happened then, that cricket is so strong now.'

Packer's personal gamble

So what of Kerry Packer? His father called him 'boofhead', but Kerry took on his family's media company and made it worth billions. There was a rumour that he once kept a Vegemite jar full of gold nuggets.

Kerry Packer was a massive gambler, even as a young man. He once placed a record million-dollar bet in Las Vegas and lost $28 million dollars in a three-week gambling spree in London. But he loved cricket and took it to the hearts and minds of millions. He encouraged experimentation with new cricket formats, like the newest kid on the block.

Twenty20

It sounds like the name of a robot, but there's nothing robotic about Twenty20 (T20) cricket. This is more of a half-day game, with each side playing just twenty overs, as the name suggests. It was first played in England in 2003, and has brought yet more excitement to the game. New rules, all approved by the ICC, the MCC and every other CC, have kept pace with this race of a game. Boundaries have been shortened to make for some great scores. The batsman gets a free hit if the bowler delivers a no-ball — another crowd-pleaser.

The first T20 international was played between England and New Zealand's women's sides in 2004. A year later, the men joined in with a match between Australia and New Zealand. Since then, it has been taken up at great speed across the cricket world, from club to first class teams. The first T20 Championship was held in South Africa in 2007, and was won by a jubilant India. Some cricket commentators believe that T20 could replace the ODI World Cup. But the ICC is determined to stick to the plan and hold the World Cup every two years, until 2012 at least.

The short and the long of it

Have the batting blasts and bright lights of the ODI and T20 blinded the cricket world? Has it weakened concentration, stamina and technique for four and five-day matches? The arguments come and go. But there is no doubt that limited-over games are often thrillers. And the International World Cup has thrown up some great surprises. It has pulled nations like Sri Lanka into the top-flight arena and given confidence to their Test game, too. It has breathed new life into old grounds and inspired many new ones.

The MCG, Melbourne, Australia during the 1936/37 MCC tour of Australia.

21 Great grounds, momentous MATCHES

On 15 March 1877, cricket history was made. And it was made at the Melbourne Cricket Ground – the legendary MCG. The first true modern international Test match was played, and between those two great rivals, Australia and England. More legendary things followed at the MCG, such as the traditional Boxing Day Tests. Like a piece of classic furniture, this ground has gathered a patina of history and shine. With other early international cricket arenas, it was the spawning ground for many new grounds across the globe.

There are now 97 Test grounds around the world. Many are old familiars, weathered into the landscape of those first test nations. But tests are now also played in countries that are still only associate or affiliate members of the ICC. Cricketers can now enjoy and endure conditions as blistering as those in Dubai in the Middle East and as lush as the spanking new Providence Stadium in Guyana, which saw it's first test ball zip across the turf on 18 March 2008.

It's a far cry from cricket played by struggling nations. In strife-torn Afghanistan, a pitch can be a dust track, its scenic view a crashed aeroplane. In 2009, cricket lovers on Vanuatu, a clutch of over 80 tiny South Pacific islands, waited with baited breath. Would the ICC approve their modest national pitch? And would that lead to Vanuatu becoming an Associate member of the ICC? Well, yes they did, and cricket dreams are coming true.

Fine features

Grounds were at first surrounded by thronging, jostling spectators. Then by the mid-19th century, a stand or two was built around a pavilion. For the well-to-do, of course. In Canada and other nations where the British Army took their cricket, great tents were put up for the ladies who lunched while the chaps chased the ball. But as the game grew globally, so too did the facilities around the grounds.

Out of sight

Large sight screens help the batsman pick out the ball against the stands. They're pulled across the boundary behind the bowler. For decades they were made of wooden slats painted white, and darker for one-day games to show up the white ball. That was all very well for the batsman, but what about the spectators faced with a wall of wood? A solution was found. In 2004, London's Lord's cricket ground trialled the first clear screen with a polycarbonate coating. At last the spectators could see through it, but the batsmen could still see the ball.

Slow scoring

Question: How many bulbs did it take to light up the first electronic cricket scoreboard?

Answer: Twenty-six for each number.

It seems like an antique now, but in 1969, the first electronic scoreboard was the height of automation and sophistication. Until then, the score was registered manually. A scorer hung numbered tiles on hooks screwed into a piece of wood. Or, at larger grounds, a handle turned numbers that rotated on rollers or a drum.

The saviour of this situation was a student, who had started a project on an electronic digital scoring device. With luck it would help him pass his 'Elements of Engineering' course at England's Wymondham College. Little did he know that two engineers, Dave Gorman and Andy Seely would see its potential and develop it into the first-ever working electronic scoreboard.

It was enormous, clumsy, covered in wires and took a lot of working hours to put together. Thank goodness for students! A pack of them spent their Sundays helping out. Rain and a waterlogged pitch delayed the scoreboard's unveiling, but the cricket world soon took notice of it, and took it on.

Packer 'drops in'

Kerry Packer's World Series Cricket circus only lasted two years, but what an impact it made! When it began in 1977, Packer was up against it. He couldn't even find a decent cricket ground. The Australian Cricket Board refused to let him use theirs. So no MCG, no Adelaide Oval, no WACA or Gabba. Packer had to use anywhere big enough for a huge crowd; from Perth's horseracing Trotting Track, to the Sydney Showground to Aussie Rules football grounds, like the VFL Park in Melbourne. But cricket requires a refined strip of turf, so Packer hired John Maley, a top groundsman from Brisbane's Gabba, to grow a few pitches in a hothouse. They were transported south and dropped into the cricket ground. The 'drop-in pitch' is now a common way of getting cricket going in a venue meant for something else. It has become a really sophisticated weapon, making for some interesting results. Tailor-made, it can bounce unevenly, with plenty of chances for the seamer or spinner for the first two or three days of a full game. Then it can calm down and become a batter's paradise through days four and five.

Nature's playground

Cricket shares its pitches with a lot of natural creatures and habits.

- Don Topley, or 'Toppers', of Essex County got chased across the outfield at Warwickshire by a dog. It was the highlight of an otherwise unusually mind-numbing first-class county championship match — the sort where you'd want to take a really good book. A 'sticky dog', by the way, is a 'sticky wicket' — a damp pitch with a crust over the top that has dried overnight. It makes the ball spin, and the batsmen hate it.

- Every kind of bird imaginable has dropped in on the

game of cricket, from peering pigeons to voracious vultures.

- Cutting a cricket ground is costly. But for Lynton, a town in the west of England, there has always been a natural solution. A hairy grinning creature with three-foot horns and sturdy yellow teeth that simply loves a field of juicy grass. Eighty-odd of these wild goats have roamed the green Devonshire valleys for centuries. But now they're proving a problem. The goats have been caught cavorting shamelessly in the outfield and pooing in front of the pavilion. A pity for a town that has twice *nearly* won the *Wisden's Cricketers' Almanac*'s award for prettiest pitch in England. There are so many 'nearlys' in cricket.

- The tree inside the Kent County cricket ground at Canterbury finally keeled over during a raging storm in 2006. Batsmen must have wept with joy. Hitting the tree gave them a four, which was okay. But the tree stopped an awful lot of sixes. Unfortunately, the dutiful groundsmen have another lime tree. Thankfully it is still only two metres tall.

- A bit too much nature appeared on the first One Day International at the Telstra ground, South Africa, in 2002. South Africa's Neil McKenzie stood well back at deep point. Australia's Steve Waugh struck a beautiful cover drive and McKenzie chased it hard. Then he stopped suddenly just short of the ball as he felt his pants falling down!

Barmy Army! Clap! Clap! Clap!

> *'It's a funny kind of month, October. For the really keen cricket fan, it's when you realise your wife left you in May.'*
> — Denis Norden (English comedy writer, performer and film critic)

Barmy and Beige

The character of a ground is moulded by its supporters. And England's Barmy Army and New Zealand's Beige Brigade are two of the most loved and loathed supporters' clubs in cricket. The Beige Brigade's motto is 'Passion, not fashion', as they sport their very dull beige gear with pride. But they do accessorise with full permed wigs, moustaches, sweatbands and fluorescent zinc sunblock. They also show a lot of leg in their seriously skimpy 'Stubbies'.

England's' Barmy Army drives many people bonkers. But they have supported their often-rather-sad team through thick and thin. They are a refreshing antidote to England's grand old guard, the 'Lobster Element' — overfed, over 'watered' and over in the posh stands at Lord's. What they all shared until 2006 was an attachment to alcohol. Fuel to the fire of spectators' high spirits and bad spirits.

Ban the can! (cha-cha-cha)

It was 1971 and the fourth test match at Australia's Sydney Cricket Ground was well under way. England's explosive fast bowler, John Snow, was in full swing. He took seven wickets for just 40 runs on a hot day matched by equally hot tempers. Australia's Graham McKenzie will never forget it. Snow blasted a bouncer. McKenzie tried to duck under it, but was too late. The ball smacked the side of his face and he staggered off the pitch, his shirt covered in blood.

John Snow looked anxious but finished his spell of bowling and took off to the boundary for a spot of fielding. It was a confrontational position to choose. Surely he could have fielded closer in? The Sydney crowd was in no mood for small talk. They booed and jeered, pulled his shirt and sent a cascade of empty beer cans onto the pitch around him. The England team rallied round their man. Cans were picked up. More cans were thrown back onto the ground. The hot day became chilled and ugly.

A missed chance

It should have been a pivotal moment. A chance to check the growing menace of drink in cricket grounds. But it took a further 35 years to tighten up on tipsy supporters. In 2006 the ICC banned spectators from bringing in their own alcohol, glass containers or metal cans in all Category A matches. These are the test matches, One-Day Internationals and so on, where tempers can run the highest. A spectator can bring in four 500 cl (centilitre) cans of beer or lager, or a 750 cl bottle of wine to a Category B match — that's anything up to a first-class match, like a state, county or other top club. But does this solve the problem? The bars are still open, and London's Lord's ground has got special licence to bring drinks in, whatever the category! But there are limits, even at Lord's: a litre of beer or a 75cl glass of wine for each spectator is all that is allowed — or else!

Momentous match

The first Test match at the Kingsmead ground in Durban was legendary. It was played in 1939, when a match could go on forever. And this one nearly did. It began on 3 March and ended in an exhausted draw on the 13th. It was only stopped so that England's players wouldn't miss their boat home! The game went backwards and forwards like the nearby ocean tides. Some say that these tides help swing bowlers move the ball in the air. But in 1939 they just didn't move it quickly enough. The 'Timeless Test' ended after this marathon, and was narrowed down to four or five days.

The greatest ground?

Is it the graceful MCG — the great Melbourne 'G' with its deep breath of history and ornate Victorian stands? Or Lord's in London, where the MCC is immortalised in memorabilia? Perhaps you'd prefer the spectacle of 120,000 supporters swaying, shrilling and jostling in Eden Gardens in Kolkata, India. Or the mighty Bullring at Johannesburg with its towering, terrifying stands. What about New Zealand's Queenstown ground that lies beside the breathtaking Lake Wakatipu which is shaped like a sleeping giant. Truly, everyone can explain why his or hers is the greatest ground for one reason or another. But perhaps this next ground has many reasons why it should be the greatest?

Sabina Park, Kingston — the jewel of Jamaica

The smell of succulent jerk chicken will certainly beguile you. The singing and drumming will entrance you. But don't be fooled, for the crowds at Sabina Park are some of the most savvy cricket supporters in the world. With the Blue Mountains to the North End and the Caribbean Sea to the South, the ground seems made in heaven. But Sabina Park's wicket is one of the hardest, fastest and most dangerous of all time.

This 'death strip' was abandoned in 1998 after just 61 balls of a test match between the West Indies and England. Yet the world's first triple century was scored here in the Park's opening test match between the West Indies and England in 1929/30. Then, Andy Sandham was the man of the moment. In the 1957/58 Test, the great Sir Garfield Sobers went one better and made a whopping 365 — a test record that stood for 36 years. And a triumph for Sabina Park.

Testing times

Sabina Park is a truly great and historic ground. But like so many in the West Indies and around the world it is struggling to pull in the crowds. Stands at Test matches are especially bare. Why? Have One Day International and Twenty20 competitions reduced cricket lovers' attention spans? Are cricket brains turning to blubber? Or are the short forms just more exciting? How can we return to the teeming crowds of the past?

Geoffrey Boycott, one-time top English batsman and rather forthright commentator just wants the ICC to LISTEN — and maybe especially to him. His answer is to roll out day-night Tests with a bit of the short-form razzmatazz. But what about the sacred red ball, some are asking? Just use a white one and change it every 35 overs, like they do in ODI, is Geoffrey's reply.

But let's not lose sight of cricket's soul. It isn't just about the great and the good and grounds that echo with the game's famous names. It is fundamentally about your own dear home turf.

Home turf

I bet J.T. and Father Ted, Ricey, Two Fags (later called 'Two Lumps' as he was out for very little and had to make the tea — with lots of sugar lumps to give the others energy), Babe Huppe and Skippy (with his short arms and big feet) love their ground more than any other. But who are they? They're cricketers who just love their game and the place it's in. They're from the Ville Rose team near Toulouse in France — a local team that has to put up with howling plateau winds. They love the game, really they do. But sometimes they're distracted by their teatime chips and peanuts blowing far away over the Massif Central.

Yes, in your heart of hearts, isn't the best ground really the one just down the track? Where you or your brother, mother, or best mate made that simply impossible two-fingered catch? Who skied a six over an apartment block, or blasted out the middle stump with the first ball? Isn't that the best pitch ever? As 'Truthful' of Fitzroy Crossing, Western Australia, blogs:

> *'A few saplings growing on the ground, the pitch warped with the tropical heat, empty tinnies scattered about ... no grass — just red pindan dirt... isn't that what country cricket's all about?'*

22 A matter of OPINION

'There was a slight interruption for... athletics.'

— RICHIE BENAUD, CRICKET COMMENTATOR, ON THE APPEARANCE OF A STREAKER.

From the 16th century, English cricket was a betting game. So there was always a lot of discussion about players and teams, both men and women's. But who would part with their money without knowing the players' form? At this early stage, players and teams were recommended by word of mouth. By the late 17th century, cricket was just appearing as the subject for newspapers.

CRICKET HITS THE SPORTS PAGES

1697 England's Foreign Post advertised a match in Sussex. Every player was to receive 50 guineas, which was an awful lot of money.

1700 The Post recorded a match between 'Gentlemen and Others' on London's Clapham Common. From this we learn that cricket had reached London from the southern countryside; that there was a lot of money involved, and that the main organisers were the upper classes — the 'Gentlemen' — who didn't mind playing 'Others', later known as 'Players'.

1718 The report of a court case shows us that challenging behaviour came early in the game. Chief Justice Pratt ordered the Chingford players of Essex County to resume their match. The players had stomped off because the other side 'had an advantage'. Sulking is not really cricket, of course. But the Chief Justice was more worried that Chingford's strop would lead to punters losing their money.

1720 Advertisements and reports for cricket matches were now commonplace. In this year, the hot news was that two London fielders were badly injured when they clashed heads. Was it this that stopped cricket reporting for a while? Or was it the crash of the South Sea Company? This massive international trading company went broke and caused an economic crisis called the South Sea Bubble. It sunk the fortunes of those who had invested so heavily in the game of cricket.

By the 19th century, the game was a subject for the gossip columns as much as for the sports pages. England's Dr W. G. Grace and Australia's Fred Spofforth made sure that cricket celebrity was here to stay. Grace even appeared in *Vanity Fair* – the *Hello* magazine of its day.

Radio rules the waves

'How many legs has a velocipede?' This is just one of many quaint, irrelevant questions sent in by listeners to a cricket radio commentary team. Adoring cricket fans deliver irrelevant gifts to the studios, too, like squidgy chocolate cake and cheese snacks. For commentators are heroes — from Australia's Richie Benaud and Bill Lawry, and West Indies' Tony Cozier to the Voice of Pakistan, Rameez Raja. And never forgetting England's late, great Brian Johnston, who wheezed with helpless laughter at any innocent gaff, especially those that were slightly rude.

Ball-by-ball cricket commentary on radio can sound impossibly dull. But in fact, every detail can be described accurately and vividly. Each type of ball delivery, batting stroke and fielding position has a name. Commentators have a whole cricket vocabulary to explain the game. They are very good at describing the conditions and atmosphere, too. So the humble radio can transport the listener to another country, an unfamiliar ground and a unique match.

Cricket commentary on the radio has been with us for a long time. So when television appeared, commentators had already learned their craft.

1922 Australia was the first country to broadcast cricket on radio. Len Watt commentated on a testimonial match for Charles Bannerman at the Sydney Cricket Ground.

1927 In England, the British Broadcasting Corporation relayed commentary on a match between Essex county and New Zealand at Leyton. The commentator was an ex-cricketer, 'Plum' Warner, who fluffed it. So F. H. Gillingham took over, but it was 'rain stop play'. He could find nothing to say, got desperate, and drearily read out the advertisements posted around the ground. Commentators had still to learn the art of spouting entertaining waffle.

1938 The first cricket matches were televised live — England against Australia at London's Lord's ground and the Kennington Oval. It included Len Hutton's world record run score of 364.

1946 Cricket continued to be televised after World War II for the next 30 years, the Australian Broadcasting Company, the BBC and others carried on with the same format and the same six fixed camera positions.

1977 Australia's Kerry Packer set up his own World Cricket Series and broadcast it on his Nine Network television company. Forget stiff camera angles and stodgy presentation. He introduced stump cameras, side cameras for run-outs, cameras facing both ends — a surprising 'first'. Day-night games brought dazzling lights. Slow-motion replays gave us all a chance to see if the batsman really was out. And for those unhappy batsmen who scored zero, cartoon Daddles the Duck quacked his way along the bottom of the screen. Then there were graphics, statistics, projections and plenty of commentators poking and nitpicking on just about everything.

Today Cricket is not only available on free-to-air TV today, you'll find it on pay-TV and even on your laptop through the wonders of broadband technology. You could probably watch cricket 24 hours a day if you wanted to.

It's not cricket!

'One of the greatest problems we face in cricket is violence. The worst example came in the Kampur International when Gautam Gambhir ran down the pitch and straight into Shahid Afridi. The ICC must be no less effective in preventing physical violence. For once this taboo is broken, it could be rapidly spread, just as sledging... has spread from international teams downwards.'

— Scyld Berry, Editor, Wisden Cricket Book.

Commentators spend a lot of time discussing cricketers' 'unsporting behaviour', to the power of politics, and racial discrimination. A recent story was hot news for a long while. It still rumbles on. Like so many cricket stories played out on a distant pitch, it threw up more questions than it did answers.

Did Harbajhan Singh racially abuse Andrew Symonds of Australia in 2008? Was Singh following on from similar taunts against Symonds from crowds in Mumbai? Did Symonds deserve it for sledging him first? Should they all just grow up? Radio and television pundits spout their views for hours.

Whatever the truth of the story, Singh was banned,

slightly, and Symonds rapped on the knuckles, gently. However, in the same year, Singh was given an 11-match ban for slapping Santha Sreesanth during one of the first Indian Players' League matches.

Indian cricket is by no means alone with this timeless problem. Dennis Lillee of Australia kicked Javed Miandad of Pakistan in a Test match in 1981 and Miandad lashed back at Lillee with his bat. He was fined and suspended for two matches. Not a great punishment, really. Perhaps if it had been more severe nearly 30 years ago, there would be more self-discipline today?

The might of the media

What every cricketer can be sure of is that every cricket crime and punishment will be broadcast. And since those early days of crackling wirelesses, cricket broadcasting has never looked back. Half-a-billion cricket lovers in India can watch an international match on television at any one time. That's how important the medium has become. But there are those who fear for a game that can now be judged by television viewers. There's the Packer technical paraphernalia plus the 'snickometer', the computer-generated trajectory imaging — we can now all be armchair umpires.

Packer's 'Circus' also put life into cricket commentating. Cricket commentators are like squabbling, squawking cockerels. These senior figures wind up each other and all those around them. Like the bantering Bill Lawry and Greg Chappell of Nine Network. Like these next two BBC favourites, Geoffrey Boycott and Jonathan Agnew...

Boycott: 'The listeners know that what we're saying isn't stupid.'

Aggers: 'Yes it is.'

Boycott: 'Speak for yourself.'

Aggers: 'I was.'

But a little 'stupidity' threaded through so much knowledge is no bad thing. It just helps the game keep moving on.

'To me, it doesn't matter how good you are. Sport is all about playing and competing. Whatever you do in cricket and in sport, enjoy it, be positive and try to win.'

— Ian Botham.

23 Cricket for KEEPS

Cricket has to keep evolving in order to survive. But not everybody can face change. Every day, a new cricket crisis hits the headlines. And the blogs babble on about every new detail of the player, pitch, catch, coach and catastrophe or cash-grabbing opportunity involved.

Just look at the latest innovation — the Twenty20 professional tournaments! Are these just money-making opportunities? Or do they take the game to new heights? Do they open up the game to a fresh audience? The Indian Cricket League set the ball rolling with a tournament in 2007. The floodgates opened for more, and a lot of comment.

'I think Twenty20 is a decadent, dumbed-down, third -rate formula for sub-prime cricket. I wouldn't therefore welcome its success.'

WILLIAM REES-MOGG (1928–). LEADING POLITICAL WRITER AND CRICKET LOVER. *THE TIMES* 21 APRIL 2008.

While Adam Gilchrist suggested Twenty20 served as a catalyst in the better management of cricket's future.

'Cricket was part of the 1900 Olympics when Great Britain beat France. With 2020 cricket here to stay, now is the time for the 10 full member nations of the [International Cricket Council] to plan for the development of the game for the next 100 years.'

ADAM GILCHRIST, BEIJING CONFIDENTIAL, AUGUST 2008.

One thing we can all agree on, is that cricket's 'new order' is a far cry from shepherds whacking a woollen ball with a crooked stick. Or milkmaids hooking a cheese with a churning paddle.

And there's no stopping it!

Cheerleaders sparkle as they weave their bodies and wave their pompoms. Sound technicians cry, 'Testing! Testing!' Film crews cluster around the stadium, waiting for the stars to burst out into the funnel of deafening spectators. So where are we? At the Yankee Stadium for a baseball battle? Or Maracana for a soccer sizzler? No. We're in Bangalore. And it's the eve of the first and already infamous IPL Twenty20 cricket match — the Indian Players League that has turned the cricketing world upside down. It's Kerry Packer all over again, but with even more razzmatazz and a whole lot more money.

Television rights have been sold for a billion dollars alone. Top-class cricketers are being lured from every test team for half a million. With money like this, who can blame them? But even more than this is that, as Australia's Martin Crowe says, 'They're playing in front of millions of people. And THAT is an addiction.'

The rest of the cricketing world erupted when IPL launched its latest cricket fiesta. Australian websites were banned from giving them the time of day. What would happen if their best players ran off to India to become superstars with super pay packets? But the Board soon warmed to the idea. Anything that might help boost interest in club and county cricket was worth a shot. So in 2008 they gave their blessing to England players wanting to join IPL teams — as long as they put England fixtures first.

Cricket in every corner

Cricket is exploding across the globe, from Africa to Afghanistan. In America, there are many enthusiasts who want to see it succeed. In New York and other major cities, cricket is seen as a great way of getting young people to work as a team. To learn discipline and a sense of fair play. Cricket clubs are spreading like melted butter. Even the celebrities are getting in on the act.

As part of the week long 'G'Day USA' festival, on 20 Jan 2008, a match was played on a small oval in a suburb of Los Angeles — the Leo Magnus Cricket Complex. There was no grandstand, no sightscreen, and no boundary fence. But there were plenty of people we know. Television presenter and one-time cricketer, Mike Whitney, stirred up England players and celebrities, who were enjoying a quick chat before they took to the pitch. Australian cricket legend, Steve Waugh, set the field. Finally they were ready. Mel Gibson tossed a coin for the start of the game and then retired to the celebrity tent and the meat pies. The game was not of the highest quality, but the publicity for cricket as a sport was.

Cricketers for the future

Kanga cricket, Kwick cricket, beach cricket. What could be easier to play? And with plastic bat and ball there's nothing to fear from all those budding fast bowlers. Then there is Table Cricket , a competitive game designed in England for cricket-loving but disabled youngsters. How will that develop?

And what is this, launched at England's new Rose Bowl Test arena in 2011? Cage Cricket?! It's the latest urban game, playable in a confined 'caged' space. Six cricketers play at any one time, each in a coloured zone. You take turns to bat, bowl, field and even umpire — and you can score points in all positions. Download your scores, share with other players and create your own league!

Yes, cricket is looking up for the young. Cricketing nations across the globe are launching kids' cricket programmes like fireworks in the night. Players past and present are getting in on the act. Sir Viv Richards' Foundation set up a Youth Development Programme on the island of Antigua. In 2010, top batsman Virender Sehwag and other distinguished Indian cricketers set up the Indian Cricket Foundation to enable young cricketers to reach their potential.

'Teams not Gangs' in London's East End is bridging the gap between youngsters through this gallant game. In every corner of the world the game is galloping ahead, and in places hard to imagine.

High in the Himalaya mountain range is the Everest Cricket Academy in the small country of Nepal. This new training centre, set in a school, has attracted a rather senior student among the young enthusiasts. He's a 35-year-old headmaster, who is learning cricket skills to take back to his own mountain school. Here, he is setting up practice nets and kitting out his pupils from his own pocket to give them a chance to take part in our amazing game.

Not the end of the world

Every nation follows its sporting heroes. What will happen when they're gone? Who will replace them? Can they ever be replaced? The panic sets in every time one of the 'greats' retires. But cricket history thrusts its bat seamlessly into the future. At its heart cricket will always be a game for everyone, everywhere. All you need is a bat, a ball and a cheering crowd.

Cricket time line

1183	First recorded account of a sport similar to today's cricket game.
1597	A court case makes reference to a game called 'creag', an early form of cricket.
1700	Cricket match announced on Clapham Common.
1744	The Laws of Cricket were codified for the first time.
1774	The Laws of Cricket are amended to include the addition of leg before wicket (LBW).
1787	MCC at Lord's is founded.
1809	First record of cricket being played in Spain.
1837	First recorded game of cricket in Singapore.
1838	The size of a cricket ball is restricted to a circumference of between 9 and 9¼ inches.
1844	First international match between Canada and USA.
1846	All-England XI team created and toured.
1851	Victoria and Tasmania play the first inter-colonial game in Sydney.
1852	The Singapore Cricket Club is founded.
1861	The first match between an English team and an Australian team at the MCG.
1864	The Wisden Cricketer's Almanac is established. Overarm bowling becomes legal.
1868	A team of indigenous Australians is the first Australian cricket team to travel overseas.

Cricket time line

1877	First cricket Test match, played between Australia and England. Australia won by 45 runs.
1879	The Sydney Riot of 1879, sparked by a controversial umpiring decision.
1881	The modern game of cricket was introduced to India as a result of British rule.
1883	The first Ashes series.
1888	The USA defeats the West Indies side in a two-innings international match.
1889	South Africa's first Test match.
1900	Only inclusion of cricket in Olympic games.
1904	The South Africans are defeated by the Irish team in Cork.
1923	The Irish Cricket Union is founded.
1928	First Test match of West Indies.
1930	First Test match for New Zealand, played against England.
1931	Size of stumps increased to 28 inches (71 cm) high from 27 (68.5 cm) and to 9 inches (22 cm) wide from 8 (20 cm) inches. Enforced in 1947.
1932	First Test match for India against England at Lord's. Also the time of the 'Bodyline series' captained by England's Douglas Jardine.
1937	First women's Test match in England against Australia.
1938	First television coverage of Test match cricket on BBC.
1939	The eight ball over is experimented with for the 1939 English season.
1946	First Test match between Australia and New Zealand.

1952	First Test match for Pakistan, who went on to defeat India.
1960	First tied Test match occurred between Australia and West Indies in Brisbane.
1971	The first One Day International is played in Melbourne between England and Australia.
1975	The Madrid Cricket Club is founded.
1977	Centenary Test is played at the MCG where Australia defeats England by 45 runs. World Series Cricket is born.
1981	Underarm bowling banned by the International Cricket Council after Trevor Chappell uses it on his final delivery to avoid a New Zealand victory.
1982	Sri Lanka's first Test match.
1985	Sri Lanka have their first Test win by defeating India.
1992	The third umpire is introduced.
1995	Muttiah Muralitharan receives seven no-ball decisions from umpire Darrell Hair in the second Test game of Sri Lanka versus Australia.
1999	First Test match win by Bangladesh when they defeated Pakistan by 64 runs.
2000	Some South African and Indian players found guilty of match fixing.
2003	Twenty20 Cup is created — first game played in England.
2005	The World XI is recognised by the ICC. First and last ICC Super Series Test and ODI competition. Australia pitted against a World X1 and won both Test and ODIs. Standards poor, crowds poorer and Freddy Flintoff reportedly said he was only there for the food.

2007 The first Men's ICC Twenty20 World Cup tournament held in South Africa. Sixteen nations took part. India won.

2009 The first Women's ICC Twenty20 World Cup tournament held in England — and England won.

2010 Some Pakistan players accused of match fixing — corruption in cricket once more raised its ugly head. Never mind the big guys. Cricket is cropping up everywhere...

2011 Vanuatu (80 islands — population 245 800), now with new pitch and ICC Associate status set up a Women's squad to play ICC East Africa Pacific Cup 2012 on home soil.

2011 Cricket Finland poised to set up women's game. Between June and July the sun never sets, so no need for floodlit pitches.

Highest Test Batting Average

Player	Career Span	Matches	Inns	NO	Runs	H/Score	Average
D.G. Bradman (Aus)	1928–1948	52	80	10	6996	334	99.94
IJL Trott (Eng)	2009–	18	30	4	1600	226	60.97
R.G. Pollock (SA)	1963–1970	23	41	4	2256	274	60.97
G.A. Headley (WI)	1930–1954	22	40	4	2190	270	60.83
H. Sutcliffe (Eng)	1924–1935	54	84	9	4555	194	60.73
E. Paynter (Eng)	1931–1939	20	31	5	1540	243	59.23
K.F. Barrington (Eng)	1955–1968	82	131	15	6806	256	58.67
E.D. Weekes (WI)	1948–1958	48	81	5	4455	207	58.61
W.R. Hammond (Eng)	1927–1947	85	140	16	7249	336	58.45
G.S. Sobers (WI)	1954–1974	93	160	21	8032	365	57.78

Top 10 Test Captains

Highest % of series won as captain

Player	Career	Matches	Won	Series	Won	% won
D. Jardine (Eng)	1931–1934	15	9	6	5	83.33
S. Pollock (SA)	2000–2003	26	14	10	8	80.00
J. Darling (Aus)	1899–1905	21	7	5	4	80.00
W. Woodfull (Aus)	1930–1934	25	14	5	4	80.00
D. Bradman (Aus)	1936–1948	24	15	5	4	80.00
Saleem Malik (Pak)	1994–1995	12	7	5	4	80.00
R. Ponting (Aus)	2004–2011	68	49	24	19	79.1
M. Taylor (Aus)	1994–1999	50	26	14	11	78.57
C. Lloyd (WI)	1974–1985	74	36	18	14	77.77
J. Brearley (Eng)	1977–1981	31	18	9	7	77.77

Ashes results list

Series	Season	Played in	English Captain	Australian Captain	Tests won by Australia	Tests won by England	Tests drawn	Series result	Ashes held by
1	1882–83	Australia	Hon. Ivo Bligh	W.L. Murdoch	1	2	0	England	England
2	1884	England		W.L. Murdoch	0	1	2	England	England
3	1884–85	Australia	A. Shrewsbury	T.P. Horan	2	3	0	England	England
4	1886	England	A.G. Steel	H.J.H. Scott	0	3	0	England	England
5	1886–87	Australia	A. Shrewsbury	P. McDonnell	0	2	0	England	England
6	1887–88	Australia	W.W. Read	P. McDonnell	0	1	0	England	England
7	1888	England	W.G. Grace	P. McDonnell	1	2	0	England	England
8	1890	England	W.G. Grace	W.L. Murdoch	0	2	0	England	England
9	1891–92	Australia	W.G. Grace	J. McC Blackham	2	1	0	Australia	Australia
10	1893	England	W.G. Grace	J. McC Blackham	0	1	2	England	England
11	1894–95	Australia	A.E. Stoddart	G. Giffen	2	3	0	England	England
12	1896	England	W.G. Grace	G.H.S. Trott	1	2	0	England	England
13	1897–98	Australia	A.E. Stoddart	G.H.S. Trott	4	1	0	Australia	Australia
14	1899	England	A.C. MacLaren	J. Darling	1	0	4	Australia	Australia
15	1901–02	Australia	A.C. MacLaren	J. Darling	4	1	0	Australia	Australia
16	1902	England	A.C. MacLaren	J. Darling	2	1	2	Australia	Australia
17	1903–04	Australia	P.F. Warner	M.A. Noble	2	3	0	England	England
18	1905	England	Hon. F.S. Jackson	J. Darling	0	2	3	England	England

Ashes results list

Series	Season	Played in	English Captain	Australian Captain	Tests won by Australia	Tests won by England	Tests drawn	Series result	Ashes held by
19	1907–08	Australia	A.O. Jones	M.A. Noble	4	1	0	Australia	Australia
20	1909	England	A.C. MacLaren	M.A. Noble	2	1	2	Australia	Australia
21	1911–12	Australia	J.W.H.T. Douglas	C. Hill	1	4	0	England	England
22	1912[3]	England	C.B. Fry	S.E. Gregory	0	1	2	England	England
23	1920–21	Australia	J.W.H.T. Douglas	W.W. Armstrong	5	0	0	Australia	Australia
24	1921	England	L.H. Tennyson	W.W. Armstrong	3	0	2	Australia	Australia
25	1924–25	Australia	A.E.R. Gilligan	H.L. Collins	4	1	0	Australia	Australia
26	1926	England	A.W. Carr	H.L. Collins	0	1	4	England	England
27	1928–29	Australia	A.P.F. Chapman	J. Ryder	1	4	0	England	England
28	1930	England	A.P.F. Chapman	W.M. Woodfull	2	1	2	Australia	Australia
29	1932–33	Australia	D.R. Jardine	W.M. Woodfull	1	4	0	England	England
30	1934	England	R.E.S. Wyatt	W.M. Woodfull	2	1	2	Australia	Australia
31	1936–37	Australia	G.O.B. Allen	D.G. Bradman	3	2	0	Australia	Australia
32	1938	England	W.R. Hammond	D.G. Bradman	1	1	2	Drawn	Australia
	1939-1946	Not played							
33	1946–47	Australia	W.R. Hammond	D.G. Bradman	3	0	2	Australia	Australia
34	1948	England	N.W.D. Yardley	D.G. Bradman	4	0	1	Australia	Australia
35	1950–51	Australia	F.R. Brown	A.L. Hassett	4	1	0	Australia	Australia

Ashes results list

Series	Season	Played in	English Captain	Australian Captain	Tests won by Australia	Tests won by England	Tests drawn	Series result	Ashes held by
36	1953	England	L. Hutton	A.L. Hassett	0	1	4	England	England
37	1954–55	Australia	L. Hutton	I.W. Johnson	1	3	1	England	England
38	1956	England	P.B.H. May	I.W. Johnson	1	2	2	England	England
39	1958–59	Australia	P.B.H. May	R. Benaud	4	0	1	Australia	Australia
40	1961	England	P.B.H. May	R. Benaud	2	1	2	Australia	Australia
41	1962–63	Australia	E.R. Dexter	R. Benaud	1	1	3	Drawn	Australia
42	1964	England	E.R. Dexter	R.B. Simpson	1	0	4	Australia	Australia
43	1965–66	Australia	M.J.K. Smith	R.B. Simpson	1	1	3	Drawn	Australia
44	1968	England	M.C. Cowdrey	W.M. Lawry	1	1	3	Drawn	Australia
45	1970–71	Australia	R. Illingworth	W.M. Lawry	0	2	4	England	England
46	1972	England	R. Illingworth	I.M. Chappell	2	2	1	Drawn	England
47	1974–75	Australia	M.H. Denness	I.M. Chappell	4	1	1	Australia	Australia
48	1975	England	A.W. Greig	I.M. Chappell	1	0	3	Australia	Australia
	1976–77*		A.W. Greig	G.S. Chappell					Australia
49	1977	England	J.M. Brearley	G.S. Chappell	0	3	2	England	England
50	1978–79	Australia	J.M. Brearley	G.N. Yallop	1	5	0	England	England
	1979–80**		J.M. Brearley	G.S. Chappell					England
	1980***		I.T. Botham	G.S. Chappell					England

Series	Season	Played in	English Captain	Australian Captain	Tests won by Australia	Tests won by England	Tests drawn	Series result	Ashes held by
51	1981	England	J.M. Brearley	K.J. Hughes	1	3	2	England	England
52	1982–83	Australia	R.G.D. Willis	G.S. Chappell	2	1	2	Australia	Australia
53	1985	England	D.I. Gower	A.R. Border	1	3	2	England	England
54	1986–87	Australia	M.W. Gatting	A.R. Border	1	2	2	England	England
	1987–88****		M.W. Gatting	A.R. Border					England
55	1989	England	D.I. Gower	A.R. Border	4	0	2	Australia	Australia
56	1990–91	Australia	G.A. Gooch	A.R. Border	3	0	2	Australia	Australia
57	1993	England	G.A. Gooch	A.R. Border	4	1	1	Australia	Australia
58	1994–95	Australia	M.A. Atherton	M.A. Taylor	3	1	1	Australia	Australia
59	1997	England	M.A. Atherton	M.A. Taylor	3	2	1	Australia	Australia
60	1998–99	Australia	A.J. Stewart	M.A. Taylor	3	1	1	Australia	Australia
61	2001	England	A.J. Stewart	S.R. Waugh	4	1	0	Australia	Australia
62	2002–03	Australia	N. Hussain	S.R. Waugh	4	1	0	Australia	Australia
63	2005	England	N. Hussain	R.T. Ponting	1	2	2	England	England
64	2006–07	Australia	A. Flintoff	R.T. Ponting	5	0	0	Australia	Australia
65	2009	England & Wales	A. Strauss	R.T. Ponting	1	2	2	England	England
66	2010	Australia	A. Strauss	R.T. Ponting	1	3	1	England	England

* A centenary commemoration test, ** more a ODI than a Test, *** Lord's for the centenary Test, **** A one-off Test to celebrate bicentenary celebrations

Index

Index